All Scripture references taken from the KJV of the Holy Bible, unless otherwise indicated.

AUTHORITY by Dr. Marlene Miles

Freshwater Press 2026

Freshwater press9@gmail.com

ISBN: 978-1-971933-25-2

Paperback Version

Table of Contents

PREFACE....6

AUTHORITY....9

WHO IS MAN? (NOT A TOY, NOT A JOKE)....20

AUTHORITY IS ENTRUSTED, NOT INHERENT....25

AUTHORITY IS LAYERED, NOT SINGULAR....29

THE MAIN TYPES OF AUTHORITY....33

KNOWLEDGE OF GOOD & EVIL....37

AUTHORITY DESTROYED, DISTORTED, & DECEIVED....41

GIVEN, NOT EARNED — BUT SUSTAINED THROUGH GOVERNANCE....46

ACTIVATED SEQUENTIALLY, NOT ALL AT ONCE....49

UNDER BEFORE OVER: THE CENTURION PRINCIPLE....52

AUTHORITY IS RARELY STOLEN — IT IS YIELDED....55

UNGOVERNED HUNGER AND BURNING THE PASSPORT....58

RELIGIOUS AUTHORITY GONE WRONG....64

FOUNDATIONS YOU DID NOT CHOOSE....66

HE FIRST DESCENDED....69

RECOGNITION, RETURN, AND RE-ALIGNMENT....72

FAITHFUL IN LITTLE: AUTHORITY RE-CONFIRMED 74
THE TYPES OF AUTHORITY MAN STEWARDS 76
SELF-GOVERNANCE AUTHORITY.......................77
RELATIONAL AUTHORITY 80
VOCATIONAL / ASSIGNMENT AUTHORITY 83
CIVIC AND SOCIAL AUTHORITY..........................86
SPIRITUAL AUTHORITY 89
AUTHORITY OVER MARRIAGE: WHY DESIRE IS NOT ENOUGH...94
SEXUAL RIGHTS IS ABOUT AUTHORITY 101
WHEN AUTHORITY IS PROTECTED, NOT DENIED 112
SYMBOLS OF AUTHORITY IN SCRIPTURE 115
A MAN UNDER AUTHORITY 119
FAVOR 122
THE GOVERNING... 126
WAITING WITHOUT CONSUMING 130
THE DIRECTION OF THE WITNESS 133
THE AUTHORITY LITMUS TEST 138
MATTHEW: TRUE RICHES 143
CONCLUSION 145
Dear Reader.. 149

AUTHORITY

PREFACE

Before we begin, let me show you something ancient that proves that authority is not a new idea. The Hebrew "age of authority" becomes evidence, credibility, structure, and validation that this is not just opinion. *What you are about to read is how people once understood life.* This is not psychology. This is not self-help. This is how God ordered human development from the beginning.

Authority is given at once, but activated in order.

In ancient Hebrew culture, a boy was not treated as a man simply because he grew older. He was recognized as a man when he was considered capable of self-governance, responsibility, covenant, accountability. Standing under the Law on his own; That is the age of authority.

Age 13, Bar Mitzvah (Son of the Commandment). At 13, a Jewish boy became Bar Mitzvah — literally, *"Son of the commandment."* This did not mean celebration of maturity, social coming-of-age, or permission to have fun. It meant that he is now personally responsible before God for his obedience to the Law.

Before this, his father covered him. After this, he stood under authority himself. This is the moment he becomes accountable, governable, responsible for his own choices. This is the first stage of authority.

At age 20, he is first counted for war, census, and contribution. In the Book of Numbers 1, men 20 years old and upward are counted for war, for census, for national responsibility.

Why 20?

By then, a man was expected to be self-governed, stable, and able to carry weight for the community. This is the age of recognized civic authority. He is no longer just responsible for himself, but he also now carries responsibility for others.

By age 30 he was considered to have full authority to serve publicly. In the Book of Numbers 4, the Levites begin priestly service at age 30.

Why?

Because by 30, a man was expected to have proven governance, relational stability, personal discipline, and covenant understanding. This is why in the Gospel of Luke 3, it says that Jesus began His ministry at about 30. This is not coincidence; it is cultural alignment. This is the age of recognized spiritual authority and public authority. It means that governance is now proven.

Hebrew culture recognized that authority comes online in layers. Authority is given all at once, but it is activated sequentially. There are multiple authorities and this book will discuss several of them. Even though a man has authorities, they are not all activated as soon as he gets them, and they are not all activated at once.

Sadly, many adults are still living at the pre-13 stage spiritually and emotionally: expecting others to still cover them. If other people are still covering them spiritually and or emotionally, then it is as though they are not maturing, not growing up. It is as though they are resisting responsibility, accountability, and self-governance.

Others are trying to operate at the 30 stage without having walked through the earlier ones, and that eventually produces collapse. In Hebrew culture, authority was not recognized by age alone, but by proven governance. A man was not treated as a man until he could be trusted under authority.

Then and now, in Hebrew culture, and in ours a person did not grow into authority by just getting older, but by becoming governable.

AUTHORITY

Power, influence, control, and authority are different and we will discuss them in this chapter for the purpose of bringing clarity to this topic. Authority is often confused with power, influence, and control but each carries a distinct meaning. This is evident in Biblical cultures and frameworks.

Power, (*dunamis*) is the raw ability or capacity to act or to enforce. Power can be physical, intellectual, or positional. Alone, it does not require legitimacy or moral grounding, but it is the means to make something happen.

Influence is the capacity to affect the thoughts, actions, or beliefs of others, often indirectly and through relationship. Influence does not require official position. It flows from character, trust, and Wisdom.

Control is another thing entirely. It is directing, managing or restraining behavior or outcomes. Control can be exercised with or without relational trust. While power, influence, and control can operate independently of trust or legitimacy, authority is always relational, accountable, and purpose-driven.

Authority is not self-generated; it is entrusted. Authority is not merely about having the means (power), the effect (influence), or the enforcement (control), but about being entrusted to steward and serve for the good of others and the fulfillment of a greater mandate.

Authority as stewardship, not domination

This book, explores what authority *actually* is — spiritually, emotionally, socially, and culturally — and how Christians (or anyone seeking grounded leadership) can understand, reclaim, and live out true authority without abuse, insecurity, or distortion.

This book dismantles toxic paradigms of power and replaces them with a rooted, Christ-centered, purpose-driven model for authority that brings liberty to self and others.

Universal longing — everyone wants agency, influence, and leadership that doesn't cost their soul. Every human being carries a longing — a God-shaped imprint — for authority. Not the loud, coercive authority of intimidation or control, but the quiet, unshakeable authority that walks in truth, loves without compromise, and stands without apology. This book is an invitation: to understand what authority *really* is, to confront what stole it from you, and to rise — fully alive — into the power you were always meant to steward.

The Bible doesn't present authority as one thing. It presents layers, spheres, and symbols of authority — all delegated, all stewarded. Following is a Biblical map, not exhaustive, but faithful. First Principle governs everything: Man does not possess authority autonomously. All human authority is delegated, layered, and accountable. Let us make man… and let them have dominion… (Genesis).

Power is capacity - the ability to produce an effect. You can have power without legitimacy. You can have power without Wisdom. You can have power without relationship. Power says, "I can." Power does not automatically mean, "I should."

Power without structure becomes volatility.

Influence is persuasion. It is the ability to shape perception or behavior. Influence does not require position. It does not require jurisdiction. It does not require accountability.

Influence says, "They listen to me." Influence can be righteous or manipulative. It is softer than power, but it is still potent.

Control is enforcement. It is the attempt to manage outcomes by constraint. Control often arises from fear, insecurity, distrust. Control says, "I must ensure this outcome." Control is usually compensatory. It tries to replace something else. Control is not inherently evil, but it is often brittle.

Authority is delegated legitimacy within defined jurisdiction. Authority says, "I am entrusted here." It does not coerce or plead; it simply **is** and it creates conditions that simply, *are*. It operates lawfully within boundaries. Authority does not require force to prove itself. It rests in assignment.

Power without authority becomes dangerous.

Influence without authority becomes manipulative.

Control without authority becomes oppressive.

But authority properly aligned will often generate appropriate power, healthy influence, and necessary restraint (not control). Authority is the stabilizer. It governs the others.

Power is force. Influence is sway. Control is grip. Authority is legitimacy. Legitimacy is the highest of the four. Because legitimacy creates sustainable order. Power fades. Influence shifts. Control exhausts.

Authority endures. Authority is the only one of the four that is inherently accountable. That makes it safer.

If one must be chosen Authority is the one you want. It acts without theatrics, without insecurity, without dominance. Just entrusted jurisdiction.

Power is capacity. Authority is jurisdiction. You can have capacity without permission. In Scripture, even the disciples in the Gospel of Luke, Chapter 9 were given *both* power and authority. That pairing is not accidental.

Power answers: *Can it be done?* Authority answers: *May it be done — and here?* Without authority, power becomes presumption.

Even Jesus said in the Book John 5 that He did nothing except what He saw the Father doing. That's power operating under authority. God-given power still requires alignment with God-given authority.

All power is capacity, but not all power is legitimate. There is physical power, intellectual power, financial power, spiritual power, and even social power.

Some is God-given; Some is acquired. Some is misused. Authority determines lawful use.

A wealthy person may have financial power. But without authority, which flows by stewardship alignment, that power can destroy. So, the category isn't "is the power God-given?" The category is, Is it governed?

Influence can lend itself to deception. Control is not desirable. Authority is perfect. Power requires Wisdom.

Influence without truth is manipulation. Control without trust is oppression. Power without Wisdom leads to destruction. Authority without humility is abuse. Authority is the most stable, but even authority requires character.

Wisdom is the governor of power. Authority is the boundary for power. Power is the tool. Influence is the echo. Control is usually the counterfeit.

If we rank these, we will see that control is the least desirable to have. It is fear-based enforcement. Influence is more neutral, but it is unstable. Power is neutral but dangerous without Wisdom. Authority is the highest when aligned and accountable

Authority is the only one that inherently implies delegation, connectivity --, relationship. It requires accountability boundary, and legitimacy. That's why it stabilizes the others.

Two are no-no's when misused: control, and deceptive influence. Power requires Wisdom. Authority requires humility and alignment. When authority governs power, and Wisdom governs both, you get sustainable order.

Culture may collapse power into one messy category, but they are different and that's why we are discussing this.

Authority is the only one of the four that **requires** relationship to exist legitimately. Control can exist without relationship; it can be imposed on strangers. Power can exist without relationship. You can have capacity whether anyone knows you or not. Influence can exist without relationship. A celebrity influences millions who don't know them. Authority implies delegation, recognition, alignment, accountability.

You cannot have legitimate authority in isolation. Authority always answers the question "By whom?" Even in Scripture. In the Gospel of Matthew 8, the centurion says, "I am a man under authority." That's relational language.

His authority exists because he stands in relationship to Rome. Authority flows through connection. It is not self-generated. That's why it feels stable. Authority is not just position. It is authorized position.

Authorization requires ongoing alignment, that is, ongoing relationship. If you are vacuuming, you can't unplug the vacuum can you? Authority is not a one-time transfer like a gift card. It is sustained through continued alignment.

A judge only has authority while seated in office. A police officer only has authority within commission. A parent has authority within relationship.

If the relationship is severed, authority weakens or shifts. That's why rebellion and abdication matter. They affect relational alignment. Authority is relational in origin and relational in maintenance. Relationship **is** the alignment.

Power can be possessed. Influence can be cultivated. Control can be imposed. Authority must be recognized and sustained within a relational structure. That's why it carries dignity. And that's why it requires humility; authority always answers upward before it governs outward.

You plug in your computer; it now has power. You put in your pin number; now that's authority. Your parent says you can use your computer for one hour; your parent is now controlling time of use. You are sleepy, curious, angry—those things may influence what you look at or do while using the device. If you are tipsy, that means you are under 'the influence' of the alcohol or a substance.

Yes — authority is the only one of those four that can be *amplified downstream*.

Power is usually proportional to the individual's capacity.

Influence is proportional to reach or persuasion. Control is proportional to force or leverage.

Authority can exceed visible personal strength because it is derivative. If someone stands under a higher authority, their visible personal size doesn't determine their jurisdiction. That's exactly what the centurion in Gospel of Matthew 8 understood. He wasn't powerful because of his physique. He was powerful because he was positioned under Rome. He recognized that Jesus operated the same way — under the Father.

Authority is scalable because it flows. It is not self-contained. That's why a small police officer can stop a massive truck. Not because of muscle, but because of recognized jurisdiction. The badge carries more than the body.

Now here's the stabilizer: Authority does not mean unlimited downstream effect. It means lawful jurisdiction within defined bounds. But yes — authority often looks smaller than it is because its source is higher than the individual. That's why Jesus in the Gospel of John 19 told Pilate, "You would have no authority over Me unless it had been given you from above." Authority is traced upward.

That's the key. If you want to assess someone's authority, you don't just look at them. You ask, Who sent them? Who backs them? What office do they occupy? What structure are they aligned with?

Authority is relationally sourced and sustained. And because it is sourced, it can exceed personal charisma, wealth, or force. That's what makes it different from power. Power radiates from the person. Authority radiates from alignment.

Authority downstream is real only within legitimate jurisdiction. Authority is the only one of the four that can look modest but carry disproportionate weight because of its source.

That's a very strong insight.

Control requires constant exertion. It must be monitored, reinforced, defended, reapplied. The moment pressure is removed, control collapses. Control is high-energy, low-stability. It is artificial structure, and it cannot rest. That's why it exhausts both the controller and the controlled.

Influence is DIY for the person being influenced. It only works if the person being influenced consents internally, knowingly or unknowingly. Influence has no enforcement. Influence has no jurisdiction. It is persuasive energy. It can be strong, but it is inherently unstable because it depends on perception, trust, mood and alignment. Influence can wane or wax; it must be refreshed. It is lighter weight than control, but still requires maintenance.

Authority does not require constant exertion. Authority is positional legitimacy. When authority speaks within its jurisdiction, things move because order recognizes order. Authority does not strain, shout, or chase. It simply stands in rightful placement. Authority "just is" within its sphere. It feels permanent compared to the others.

Power belongs to God. (Psalms 62:11)

Humans can possess derivative power. Power is capacity — energy, ability, force. Power is not self-legitimating. Authority governs the lawful use of Power. Power is force; Authority is order.

Power can exist without order. Authority defines the boundaries of force. That's why power without authority becomes chaos. Authority without power becomes symbolic only.

Jesus in the Gospel of Matthew 28:18says, "All authority has been given to Me." Notice He doesn't say "all power." Authority is the higher legal category. Power flows through authority.

Control is temporary. It requires high exertion Influence is also temporary, and is perception-dependent Power is real but requires governance. Authority is stable within jurisdiction.

Authority is the only one that does not require strain to sustain itself. It requires alignment, but not constant force. That's why it feels weighty. You're identifying that authority is not kinetic. It's positional.

And that's why it's desirable.

Man does not possess authority autonomously. All human authority is delegated, layered, and accountable. "Let us make man… and let them have dominion." Genesis Dominion is assigned, not inherent. **Authority** must be understood *again* identity alone is incomplete Authority is not power, but misuse leads to loss, and fear of authority dominate modern life

People generally reject toxic power and crave true authority. Faith + function —spiritual truth with real-world application.

When God made man, He didn't say let's make him and cut him loose and see what he'll do. NO, man is made for connection with God, for relationship and for authority.

WHO IS MAN? (NOT A TOY, NOT A JOKE)

Most people spend years asking, *"Who am I?"* Far fewer ever ask, *"Why does my life carry weight?"* We talk about identity as if it is a personality exercise. We ask what we like, what we prefer, what we feel called to do. But beneath all of that is a quieter, heavier truth most people sense but cannot name:

What I do matters more than I thought.

Words echo. Choices linger. Moments repeat themselves in ways we did not expect. Some decisions follow us for years, while others seem to vanish. Some people move through life lightly, as if nothing sticks to them. Others carry a gravity they never asked for.

At some point, the question changes. It is no longer: *Who am I?* It becomes: *What has been placed in my hands?* That question is where authority begins. When God sees that He can trust you; He puts things under your stewardship.

There is a reason human beings feel the weight of regret. There is a reason we say, "I wish I had known." There is a reason responsibility exists in every culture on Earth. These are not social inventions. They are signals.

They point to a truth that predates us: Man was not created to drift.

From the beginning, man is described as being given something to tend, something to name, something to steward.

Let us make man… and let them have dominion…
(Genesis 1)

Dominion is not about ruling. It is about caring for what is not originally yours. That is the first hint that man is not casual; he is entrusted.

The problem is that many people sense the weight of their lives without understanding why. They feel responsibility without framework. They feel consequences without clarity. They feel pressure without knowing what they are holding.

So, they do one of two things: They either treat life lightly, as if nothing matters, or they treat life anxiously, as if everything is fragile. Both reactions come from the same misunderstanding: They do not know what has been entrusted to them.

Many people now say *who they are* …but still don't know what they are entrusted with. They have identity language but need governance consciousness. Else, they still live like toys, grasshoppers, victims of circumstance, emotional dependents, spectators of their own lives, because they were never taught authority as stewardship.

A person who understands authority cannot live like a joke. They may fail — but they mustn't live unseriously. *Man is not a joke, a toy, a plaything, a grasshopper, or frivolous* — because man is entrusted with glory, honor, dominion, authority and so much more.

Man is not inferior. He is not designed to be a victim, or be helpless. Without shaming anyone. We are living in a time where people know their "worth" but not their weight. know their "value" but not their jurisdiction. know their "identity" but not their accountability. This book restores sobriety to being human. Not heaviness--, sobriety.

Before understanding authority, we have to stop thinking that men are grasshoppers, accidents, jokes, toys, or ornamental beings. Identity teaching which was started years ago in the Church was the rescue from self-contempt. You are not small because you are insignificant. You are small because you are *precise*. God does not entrust dominion to toys.

You are not a joke. You are not a toy. You are not an accident. You are not a grasshopper scrambling through a giant world hoping not to be noticed. You were designed with capacity. And capacity always implies expectation--not harsh expectation, not performance, but purpose.

If a cup holds water, it was made to hold something. If hands can build, they were made to steward something. If a voice can speak, it was made to affect something. Capacity is evidence of entrustment.

This is why human beings feel the sting of failure so deeply. It is not just embarrassment. It is not just social shame; it is the quiet recognition that: *I mishandled something that mattered.* That recognition is the doorway into understanding authority. Because authority is not first about what you can command, it is about what you were trusted with.

Before we can talk about authority in families, in work, in marriage, in leadership, or in the spiritual realm, we must first settle this: Your life is not lightweight. It has consequence because it has been entrusted with something. You may not yet know what that is. But you have felt it. Every person has.

That feeling is not accidental. It is the first whisper of authority. And until a person understands that they have been entrusted, they will never understand why their life feels heavy in moments that should feel small.

You were given something to steward. Identity tells a man who he is. Authority tells him why his life is not casual.

We start at **weight**.

Who has a thoroughbred and doesn't race it. Who has a muscle car and doesn't rev the engine? design implies intent. Capacity implies expectation. No one builds torque without load, speed without destination, or strength without resistance. So, when Scripture asks *"Who is man?"* It is really asking: Why is man engineered for weight?

What is man, that Thou art mindful of him?
Book of Psalms 8

David is stunned. He's looking at celestial bodies in their majestic order. Then he is considering man, fragile, limited, dust-made. The real question is not *value*; it's **appointment**. *Why would God entrust so much to something so small?*

That is the terror and glory of being human.

You must ***be*** before you can lead. True leadership is built on foundation of self-awareness and authenticity. So who are you? This means coming to terms with your values, beliefs, and unique design. Authority is not simply a function of position or title; it flows from a secure sense of identity. When you know who you are, you lead with confidence, integrity, and clarity.

Authority is rooted in identity, not performance. Many people believe authority is earned solely through achievement or demonstrated ability, but lasting authority is not the fruit of performance alone. Instead, it is grounded in the recognition of what has been entrusted to you—your calling, gifts, and character. Performance may open doors, but identity sustains influence. When your authority is rooted in your authentic self rather than external validation, you lead from a place of stability and purpose, not anxiety or fear of failure. This inner alignment is what allows authority to be exercised wisely and for the good of others.

AUTHORITY IS ENTRUSTED, NOT INHERENT

Scripture does not treat authority as one monolithic thing. It treats it as distinct stewardships. Authority is entrusted, not inherent because even inherited authority comes from God. flows through structure. can be revoked. can be diminished. can be bypassed. No human *possesses* Divine authority in themselves.

Even Jesus says:

> All authority has been given to Me…
> (Matthew 28)

Authority is entrusted, not inherent. Even when authority is inherited, it is still received — never self-originating — and must be governed to be retained. Inheritance may grant position, but authority remains delegated and accountable."

This distinction explains why heirs can fail, why dynasties collapse, why some people "have everything" but no Peace, why authority leaks despite advantage. It does so without shaming inheritance. Inheritance is not the problem. Ungoverned inheritance is. Inheritance increases responsibility, not security. That's why

Scripture say, *"To whom much is given..."* Inherited authority raises the standard — it does not lower it.

If man is entrusted, then a natural question follows: Where did this entrustment come from**?** one thing becomes immediately clear, human beings do not generate authority on their own. We do not wake up one day and decide that our lives matter. We do not invent responsibility. We do not create consequence.

These things were here before us. That is the first clue that authority is not inherent to man. It is **given** to him. There is a difference between something you possess and something you are trusted with. You possess what belongs to you. You steward what belongs to another. From the very beginning, man is described not as an owner, but as a steward.

"Let us make man… and let them have dominion…" Dominion is often misunderstood. It is imagined as control, power, or rule. In its simplest sense, **means** to care for what is not originally yours. The Earth was not man's creation. Life was not man's invention. Order was not man's design, yet man was placed in the middle of it and told to tend it. That is entrustment.

This is why authority feels heavy; it is not self-created. You feel the weight of it because it did not originate with you. It was placed in your hands. Authority that originates from self is called ego. Authority that is entrusted is called stewardship. And the difference between the two is everything.

This is also where autonomy is often misunderstood. Many people assume autonomy means independence from all authority. But true autonomy is simply the ability to stand and choose within the authority structure you are already under. You cannot step outside authority, because you did not create it. You only align with it or resist it.

This is why rebellion never produces Peace. It attempts to stand outside a structure that existed before you arrived. Even when authority appears to be inherited — through family, position, role, or opportunity, it is still not self-originating.

Inheritance may grant access. It does not grant ownership. A person may inherit position, but they must still steward authority. History is filled with people who inherited much and governed little.

That is because authority is never owned; It is always held in trust. Understanding this removes two common distortions. First, it removes pride. If authority is entrusted, then there is nothing to boast about. You did not invent what you were given. Second, it removes inferiority. If authority is entrusted, then your life carries weight whether you feel worthy or not. Both arrogance and self-contempt dissolve here. Both are based on the false idea that authority comes from self.

Dominion was never a license to control. It was a call to steward and that implies accountability. You are not powerful because you are impressive. You are responsible because you have been trusted. That is a very different kind of weight.

This is why people often feel uncomfortable around the word authority. They associate it with domination, abuse, or control. Biblical authority began in a garden, not a throne room. It begins with tending, naming, caring, and cultivating.

Authority begins not with ruling others, but with caring for what has been placed within reach. When you understand that authority is entrusted, not inherent, something settles inside you. You stop trying to prove yourself. You stop trying to escape responsibility.

You realize that your life carries weight because you were trusted with something long before you understood what it was. that realization is not frightening, it is steadying. what is entrusted can be learned, governed and if necessary, restored. But first understand: It was never yours to own. It was always yours to steward.

AUTHORITY IS LAYERED, NOT SINGULAR

Many people think of authority as a single thing. You either "have it" or you "don't." You either feel powerful or you feel powerless. You either are responsible or you are not. But Scripture does not treat authority that way, and neither does real life.

Authority is not singular. It is layered. That is why when something goes wrong in one part of life, it rarely stays there. A person may say, "I don't know what happened. Everything seemed to fall apart at once."

A relationship struggles. Work becomes unstable. Peace disappears. Clarity fades. Confidence drops. It feels mysterious. Sudden. Unexplainable. But what is actually happening is this. A lower layer of authority weakened, and the layers above it began to feel the strain. Because authority is integrated.

Consider something simple. If a person cannot govern their own appetite, it eventually affects their relationships, their finances, their work, their peace, their decision-making. Not because those things are directly related to appetite, but because the same person stands in all of those places.

When self-governance weakens, every other form of authority begins to wobble. This is why Scripture speaks so often about small things. Speech. Temper. Restraint. Patience. Obedience.

These seem minor, but they are not. They are load-bearing. They sit at the lowest layer of authority — the authority of self-governance — and everything else rests on them. You do not step into relational authority without self-governance. You do not carry vocational authority without self-governance. You do not sustain spiritual authority without self-governance.

When this layer cracks, the others do not immediately collapse — but they begin to weaken.

That is why people often say "I don't know why this affected everything." Because they were looking for a single cause in a single area, not realizing authority functions as a system.

Authority in man can be understood in layers.

At the base is self-governance. Above that is relational authority. Above that is functional or vocational authority. Above that is influence and spiritual authority. These are not separate compartments. They are connected. You carry the same person into all of them. This explains something many people experience but cannot explain, Why a struggle in private eventually appears in public. Why internal disorder eventually becomes external instability. Why unresolved issues eventually touch everything.

It is not because life is unfair. It is because authority is integrated. This is also why restoration must begin at the lowest layer. People often try to fix the visible problems. First they attempt to repair the relationship, change the job, improve the image, speak with more confidence. But if self-governance is still weak, those repairs do not hold.

The weight returns, and the same patterns reappear. Because you cannot stabilize the upper layers while the foundation remains cracked. Understanding that authority is layered does something important. It removes confusion.

You stop asking, "Why is everything affected?" And start asking, "Where did governance first weaken?" That question is not condemning; it is clarifying. If you know where the strain began, you know where restoration must begin.

This is why authority cannot be treated as a single trait or a personality quality.

It is not something you either possess or lack. It is something you steward across multiple layers of your life. And the health of each layer affects the others, whether you notice it or not.

Once you see this, many experiences begin to make sense. You begin to understand. Why peace leaks. Why confidence wavers. Why decisions feel harder than they should. Why small habits matter more than you thought. Because you are not living in separate compartments.

You are carrying one integrated authority across every part of your life. And that realization is not heavy. It is relieving. Because now you know: You do not have to fix everything at once.

You begin where authority always begins — with the layer closest to you.

THE MAIN TYPES OF AUTHORITY

1. Self-Governance Authority
   (Primary, foundational)
   – Appetite
   – Speech
   – Boundaries
   – Obedience
2. Relational Authority
   – Marriage
   – Family
   – Generational stewardship
3. Vocational / Functional Authority
   – Assignment-based
   – Offices, mantles, roles
4. Civic / Social Authority
   – Government
   – Law
   – Social recognition
5. Spiritual Authority
   – Authority in the unseen realm
   – Operates through alignment and obedience

Self-governance is the load-bearing authority. All others rest on it.

Some authority *is* inherited. The key is *how* it is inherited and *what kind* it is.

1. **Authority Over Creation (Dominion).** This was given in Eden. Man was given stewardship over the Earth. He named animals. He was assigned to cultivate and keep the ground as well as govern the environment, not exploit it. Status: *Fractured*, not erased, after the Fall

2. Authority of Self-Governance (Foundational, Often Ignored). This is the authority Scripture **assumes**, discipline, appetite control, Obedience, and moral agency. This is done through fasting, restraint, and boundaries. When self-governance collapses, every other authority eventually fails.

This is why Jesus begins with appetite in the wilderness — not miracles.

3. Relational Authority within **ordered relationships** such as marriage, family, generational blessing, and household governance. We see this in fatherhood, headship, and covering. When this authority is **abused or abdicated**, disorder multiplies generationally.

4. Vocational / Functional Authority. Authority tied to **assignment**, not identity. Kings rule. Priests mediate. Prophets speak. Elders govern. Judges decide. When assignment ends, authority ends — unless it has been seized illegitimately. We are talking about legitimate authority even though false authority can exist.

5. Civic / Legal Authority. Scripture acknowledges governmental authority even when rulers are flawed. There is no authority except from God...(Romans 13). Symbols are the Throne, Scepter, Law, Seal Are all *acknowledgments*, not endorsement.

6. Spiritual Authority – authority in the unseen Realm. This authority was delegated to Adam. It was distorted at the Fall. It was restored through Christ.

I give you authority...(Luke 10). Symbols of this authority are the Name, Word, Command. Spiritual authority flows through alignment, not volume.

Is authority inherited? Yes — but never autonomously. Inherited authority is still delegated authority, just delegated through lineage or covenant, not directly to the individual. Authority can be inherited, but it is never self-originating. Inheritance does not mean: self-generated, guaranteed, unaccountable, or permanent. It means entrusted through position, recognized through lineage, confirmed through stewardship.

Scripture shows three primary kinds of inheritance-related authority:

1. Inherited Jurisdiction – this is position without proven character. Examples: Kingship passed through bloodlines. Priesthood through tribe. Land inheritance. Family authority structures. Saul's house, Eli's sons,

Rehoboam. They *receive position* —but must prove governance. This is why inherited authority is the *most vulnerable* to collapse. Inheritance grants access, not immunity.

2. Covenantal Inheritance (promise-based authority). *God said.* Examples:

- Abraham → Isaac → Jacob
- Davidic covenant
- Tribal blessings

Here, authority is promised by God, passed generationally, conditional on alignment. The covenant continues —but individuals can be cut off from its benefits. David's throne stands; some of David's sons do not.

3. **Spiritual Inheritance** is about capacity, not control. Spiritual inheritance includes callings, sensitivities, inclinations, capacities. But capacity is not authority until governed. A child may inherit prophetic sensitivity, leadership presence, spiritual awareness. If unguided, that inheritance becomes instability, misuse, pride, confusion. Scripture never treats spiritual inheritance as automatic authority.

KNOWLEDGE OF GOOD & EVIL

(Order, Not Earning)

The Bible shows many instances of personal authority sabotage. Primarily stepping out of alignment with God by stepping into sin. Once out from under authority, the sinner will see his authority no longer flows. The first sin shows this clearly.

Have you ever wondered if Adam and Eve were getting the 'knowledge of good and evil', then how did they make such an uninformed choice to trade authority for 'fruit"? The knowledge they received was real, but it was premature, unintegrated, and ungoverned. That's why the choice looks uninformed even though it involved "knowledge."

What *kind* of knowledge was "the knowledge of good and evil"? In the Book of Genesis 2–3, "knowledge" does not mean Wisdom, maturity, discernment, or authority. It means experiential awareness, empirical knowledge. In Hebrew thought, *to know* is not to understand abstractly — it is to enter into experience. So "the knowledge of good and evil" is not knowing what good and evil *are, i*t is bearing internal awareness of both, without governance. It is without governance because they were not submitted to God, as a matter of fact they were disobedient and stepping out of alignment at the time.

Why the choice wasn't "informed" despite the knowledge Adam and Eve did not trade authority *after* understanding the cost. They traded authority before they had the capacity to govern what they were receiving.

They already had innocence, alignment, authority, covering, and access. What they *lacked* was tested discernment, consequence-bearing wisdom, restraint under pressure. So, the temptation wasn't, "Do you want evil?" No, it was, "Do you want access without waiting?"

That's appetite, not ignorance.

What the knowledge actually gave them (immediately). Notice what Scripture says happened right away. Their eyes were opened. They became self-conscious. They experienced shame. They hid. They covered themselves. That tells us the knowledge was relational and internal, not cosmic or governmental.

They did not gain authority, Wisdom, rule, or dominion. They gained self-awareness without covering, moral consciousness without governance, nor perception without capacity. That's why the knowledge is destabilizing.

Was this "second heaven" knowledge? Well, lets compare this 'temptation' to the temptations of Jesus in the Wilderness...

Not in the way people usually mean it. This was not angelic knowledge, celestial administration, cosmic governance, heavenly secrets. It was fallen experiential knowledge — awareness produced by *disobedience*, not assignment.

If we were to place it in a framework, it's closer to: earthly consciousness corrupted by autonomy. Not second-heaven authority — but unshielded perception.

That's why Scripture later says, "Be wise in what is good, and innocent in what is evil."

In other words: *do not gain evil through experience.*

Fruit seemed to outweigh authority in that moment in Eden. Because authority is invisible, and fruit is seen, visible, and immediate. They did not understand authority as something that could be lost — because they had never seen loss.

So, the trade wasn't calculated. It was unguarded. They didn't say "Let's give this up." They said (implicitly) "Surely this won't cost us." That's not informed rebellion. That's immaturity encountering appetite. Adam and Eve did not lack information. They lacked governance capacity.

They gained knowledge before restraint. Awareness before Wisdom. Perception before authority was tested. Cart before horse. That's why the knowledge didn't elevate them; it destabilized them. They did not gain forbidden information they gained awareness they were not yet governed enough to carry.

When a person in in sin or has sin guilt, they disqualify themselves b not participating or not getting back into alignment to return under authority. God forgives, but when we do not forgive ourselves, we turn down many blessings of God, as well as not making ourselves available to authority. Sin-guilt, shame, trauma and shrinking away from the presence and alignment with God are both self-disqualifiers.

People-pleasing as jurisdiction surrender. Do not excessively thank them for basic decency. Sure you have manners, but don't be excessive. Avoid saying "Thank you so much for giving me a chance." Say it once if you must but don't grovel. "I can't believe you chose me." if you're a kid and this is your first job ever, that may come out of your mouth, but those words are signals to opportunists who want to take advantage of people. Over-gratitude subtly frames you as indebted. A Pharaoh mentality doesn't have a heart of flesh: he has a hardened heart and he hears gratitude as: *"This person will tolerate pressure, delay, or control."* At that point the person has stepped out from under authority.

Chronic apology over-humbles a person and leads to authority leakage. That's the pattern.

AUTHORITY DESTROYED, DISTORTED, & DECEIVED

Across societies, authority is often organized around visible and invisible lines--, gender, race, socioeconomic status, and entrenched hierarchies. These structures intended to bring order and instead become barriers that limit opportunity silence voices and foster division for example gender-based authority can marginalize women or non-binary individuals relegating them to roles with less influence or fewer resources Hierarchies may create environments where certain groups are systematically disadvantaged or excluded, perpetrating cycles of inequality and injustice.

Status and class distinctions can further entrench privilege, making authority less about stewardship and more about power and control. These systemic hierarchies openly shape institutions and relationships.

Authority can become oppressive when it doesn't serve or steward, but instead it silences or exploits. Authority can be abused to maintain power at the expense of others. We can see this in legalism, manipulation, or rituals that may claim to be Christian or Godly, but they may be leaning toward other 'religious' practices.

Recognizing harmful patterns can help a person get back on the right track to restored authority.

Dominion is assigned. Core authorities are given to man. (These were listed previously.)

1. **Authority Over Creation** (Dominion) given in Eden.

2. **Authority of Self-Governance**

3. **Relational Authority**

4. **Vocational / Functional Authority** tied to assignment.

5. **Civic / Legal Authority.**

6. **Spiritual Authority** in the unseen realm. Delegated to Adam. Distorted at the fall Restored through Christ

The devil's core distraction set is food/provision. At Eden, he tricked them to take fruit before obedience. In the Wilderness there were manna complaints and craving for Egypt's food. Esau traded his birthright for stew. The appetite for food displaces patience, inheritance, authority, usually not suddenly, but over time.

Modern day devil distractions are: Money anxiety, Job panic, "I can't afford to obey God." Survival-first decision making destroys authority alignment. Provision anxiety is the fastest way to reroute authority.

Sex sins can destroy authority. In the Bible we see David & Bathsheba. Samson & Delilah. Moabite women with Israel (Numbers 25). This displaces discernment, restraint, covenant, and spiritual awareness.

Situationships, pornography, emotional affairs, validation-seeking intimacy all distort and destroy authority alignment.

Illicit intimacy trades long-term covering for short-term satisfaction.

Comfort and ease threaten authority. In the Bible, the Israelites wanted to return to Egypt's familiarity, even though it was slavery. Lot choosing the well-watered plain. Peter resisted the cross when Jesus said that is what must happen. (*Far be it from You,* (Mtt 16:22)). These acts displaced obedience, growth, and calling.

Modern day avoidance of hard obedience includes fear of discomfort and staying where things are known and familiar, even if that place is stagnant.

Comfort delays transformation more quietly than suffering.

Fear of the enemy is a real enemy. In the Bible, Israel's refusing to enter Canaan. Saul sparing Agag. The Disciples fleeing at arrest. This displaces courage, trust, and movement. In modern day terms, that's fear of loss, fear of rejection, and fear of instability. Fear convinces a person to lay down authority.

Being focused on status and the approval of people threatens authority. Saul needed people's approval. Pharisees loved praise. Herod and Haman both wanted honor. This displaces obedience, integrity, and truth-telling. In modern terms: Image management, Platform dependency, and people-pleasing. When approval governs, authority becomes performative.

Urgency distorts authority. Saul offering sacrifice "because time was running out." Sarah put Abraham with Hagar to try to create an heir. Jacob & Esau's rushed exchange. It displaces waiting, trust, and God's timing. Modern "I can't wait" decisions. Panic moves, and shortcuts. Urgency is really appetite dressed as necessity.

Seeking knowledge and insight without submission in the Bible. The Tree of Knowledge. Simon Magus wanting power. Demons knowing Jesus but not obeying Him. All this displaces Wisdom, submission, and reverence. Modern spiritual information addiction, theory without obedience, and analysis paralysis all distort authority. Knowledge without submission inflates confidence but erodes authority.

The devil does not distract with evil first; he distracts with legitimate needs at illegitimate times. Food. Sex. Safety. Belonging. Understanding. All are presented by the devil to interrupt governance.

These still work today because human biology hasn't changed. Attention is still finite. Authority still requires presence, and appetite still speaks loudly when unattended.

What you attend to governs what you yield. The enemy rarely steals authority — he distracts it into dormancy. Authority is not overpowered; it is out-attended. What repeatedly interrupts governance is not random — it is strategic.

The devil doesn't need to defeat authority, he just needs to keep it busy elsewhere, distract a person or entice him to lay authority down. Every one of these distractions is still operating today, because they target human attention, not ancient culture.

GIVEN, NOT EARNED — BUT SUSTAINED THROUGH GOVERNANCE

One of the most confusing ideas about authority is the belief that it must be earned. People assume authority comes from experience, age, effort, intelligence, or success. Scripture never presents authority that way. Authority is not awarded for performance. **It is given as a trust.**

From the beginning, man is given dominion before he has done anything to deserve it.

> Let us make man… and let them have dominion…(Genesis 1)

Man appears to have no qualifications. There were no tests and no proof of ability. Dominion is entrusted simply because man was created. That is the first thing to understand: Authority is a gift before it is a responsibility.

This removes a common burden. You do not have to prove yourself worthy of authority. You already live inside it. Your life already carries consequence. Your words already carry weight. Your choices already affect more than you realize. Authority is present whether you acknowledge it or not.

But this is where confusion often arises. If authority is given and not earned, why do some people seem to have more of it than others? The answer is not that they were given more. It is that they stewarded what they were given more carefully. Authority is given freely, but it is sustained through governance.

Think of authority like a trust placed into your hands. You did not earn it, but you are responsible for how it is handled. Over time, faithful stewardship causes authority to expand. Neglect or misuse causes authority to diminish. Not because God retracts it in anger, but because authority responds to governance.

Jesus describes this principle plainly, He who is faithful in little is faithful also in much…(Luke 16)

That statement is not about money. It is about authority. Faithfulness does not earn authority. It reveals that authority can be trusted in your hands. This is why people often feel stuck. They think they must achieve something before authority can increase. But authority does not respond to achievement. It responds to governance. How you handle your words, your time, your appetites, your reactions, and small responsibilities determines how much authority can safely rest with you.

This is also why authority is not theatrical. You rarely notice it growing. You simply notice that decisions feel clearer, Peace feels steadier, influence feels natural, trust increases. Authority expands quietly because governance is quiet.

Understanding this removes both pride and discouragement. You cannot boast about authority, because you did not earn it. You do not have to despair about authority, because you can steward it. That is the Mercy in this design.

Authority is not something you chase. It is something you care for. And the more carefully you care for it, the more room it has to operate. This is not about impressing anyone. It is about becoming a person who can be trusted with what they have already been given.

When you see authority this way, life becomes less about striving and more about stewardship. You stop asking, "How do I get more authority?" And start asking, "How well am I governing what is already in my hands?" That is an indication as to how much authority can safely rest with you next.

Authority is given. But it is sustained, strengthened, and expanded through governance.

ACTIVATED SEQUENTIALLY, NOT ALL AT ONCE

Authority is given at once. But it is not activated at once. many people feel discouraged by comparing their present capacity to what they believe they should already be able to carry. They assume that because authority exists in their lives, it should function fully in every area immediately. But authority comes online **in order**.

From the beginning, man is entrusted with dominion, but he does not immediately govern everything. He first tends the garden. He names what is in front of him. He learns stewardship in the space closest to him.

Authority begins near, not far. This pattern continues throughout Scripture and throughout life. A person first learns to govern themselves. Then they learn to govern relationships. Then they learn to carry responsibility. Then they learn to influence beyond themselves.

Each layer prepares the next. This is not delay. This is protection.

Many people feel frustrated because they sense the weight of authority but cannot yet express it in the ways they imagine. They want to lead before they can govern themselves. They want influence before they have steadiness. They want responsibility before they have restraint. But authority cannot safely operate out of order. When it is rushed, it collapses.

This is why Scripture emphasizes faithfulness in small things. Small does not mean unimportant. Small means **foundational**. The way you handle what is nearest to you determines what can be trusted to you next. If authority were activated all at once, many lives would break under the weight. Instead, it comes online gradually, as governance grows.

This explains something many people experience but misinterpret. They feel capable. They feel called. They feel ready. But their life does not yet reflect the level of authority they sense inside. That is not rejection. It is sequence. Authority is waiting for governance to mature enough to support it.

Rushing authority produces collapse because it places weight on layers that are not yet strengthened. This is why people often experience early success followed by sudden failure, quick influence followed by instability, responsibility that feels overwhelming. They were not wrong to step forward. They were simply ahead of their own order.

Authority that arrives too quickly feels exciting.

Authority that arrives in order feels steady. The first produces drama. The second produces endurance. And endurance is the goal.

Understanding this removes impatience. You stop asking, "Why isn't this happening yet?" And begin asking, "What is still being strengthened in me?" That question keeps you aligned with the process instead of fighting it.

Authority is not withheld to frustrate you. It is activated sequentially to protect you. Because authority that comes in order does not collapse when weight is added. It holds. And when it holds, you are able to carry what has been entrusted to you without fear, panic, or performance.

Authority is given all at once. But it is activated in order. And that order is one of the greatest mercies in how God entrusts man.

UNDER BEFORE OVER: THE CENTURION PRINCIPLE

One of the clearest explanations of how authority functions comes from a man who did not belong to Israel, did not hold a religious office, and did not speak from theology. He spoke from experience.

I am a man under authority, having soldiers under me. I say to one, 'Go,' and he goes… Gospel of Matthew 8

This man understood something many people miss:

Authority does not begin with what is under you. It begins with what you are properly under. The centurion was not impressed by Jesus' power. He recognized Jesus' order. He understood that Jesus did not need to be physically present, did not need to exert effort, and did not need to supervise the outcome. Because he understood how authority moves when alignment is correct. Authority travels through structure.

People can misunderstand authority, here. They focus on what they can command. They focus on influence, leadership, voice, or position. But the centurion reveals that the true source of authority is not outward.

It is alignment. To be “under authority” is not humiliation. It is positioning. It means you are standing in the current of order instead of outside it. It means you recognize that authority flows from somewhere greater than you, and you willingly remain within that structure.

That alignment is an intangible power. When a person steps outside of proper order, something subtle happens. Their words require more effort. Their influence requires more force. Their decisions carry less weight. They begin trying to produce results through personality instead of order.

That is exhausting. And it is unnecessary.

The centurion did not raise his voice. He did not explain himself. He did not argue. He simply said, in effect: “I understand how this works.” And Jesus marveled. Not at his faith alone — but at his understanding of authority.

This is why many people feel frustrated in their attempts to lead, influence, or speak with weight.

They are trying to exercise authority without first examining what they are standing **under**. Authority does not flow through independence. It flows through alignment. Being **under** is not weakness.

It is what allows authority to function without strain. A person who is properly aligned does not need to perform authority. They simply carry it.

This explains why some people seem calm and effective without effort, while others strain and push without results. It is not personality. It is order. One is standing within it. The other is trying to recreate it.

The centurion teaches us something vital: Authority is not proven by what responds to you. It is proven by what you are properly aligned under. That alignment is invisible, but its effects are unmistakable. Understanding this changes how you think about authority entirely.

You stop asking, "How do I gain more authority?" And begin asking, "Where am I standing?" Because when you are properly positioned, authority flows naturally through you. Without force. Without performance. Without strain. Authority does not begin with being over. It begins with being under. And that is one of the most powerful, overlooked truths about how authority actually works.

And as a point of reset, in the natural authority is earned by merit as in the workplace, but in the system of God authority is given and it works incrementally and by steps and stages according to the will of God and the man who carries that authority.

AUTHORITY IS RARELY STOLEN — IT IS YIELDED

Most people do not wake up one day and decide to give their authority away. They do not announce it. They may not even recognize when it has faded or is gone. They do not even realize when it is happening. Over time, they may begin to feel something has shifted. Peace is harder to hold. Decisions feel heavier. Clarity fades. Confidence weakens.

Authority has been yielded.

They often say, "I don't know when things changed. I just know they did." That is because authority is rarely stolen. It is **yielded**.

Scripture rarely shows dramatic moments where a person loses authority in a single act. Instead, it shows a pattern of small decisions--, first one compromise under pressure, then one silence to avoid conflict. One appetite placed above discernment; one boundary blurred. One "just this once" are common ways authority can be yielded. None of these feel catastrophic at the time, but authority is not lost ceremonially; it is laid down gradually.

This is what makes the loss of authority so confusing. You cannot point to a single moment. You cannot identify a clear exchange. You simply wake up one day realizing you are no longer standing where you once stood.

Authority is not an object that can be handed over like keys. It is relational and functional. You do not give it away. You **defer it**. To fear. To comfort. To approval. To appetite. To survival. And whatever you defer to begins to decide for you. That is governance transfer.

Imagine leaving a coat somewhere years ago and not remembering when or where. You did not throw it away. You did not mean to lose it. You simply set it down, walked away, and never realized it was gone until the cold reminded you. That is how authority is often lost. Not through rebellion. Through inattention.

Scripture treats this gently but clearly. Authority is lost through neglect, misplaced trust, prolonged compromise, abdication rather than defiance. This is important because it means something hopeful. If authority were stolen, recovery would require force. Because it was yielded, recovery requires **recognition and return**.

Many people carry unnecessary shame because they assume they must have done something dramatic to lose their footing. Often, they did not. They simply stopped governing small things, and over time, the effects spread. This is not condemnation, it is clarity.

When you understand that authority is yielded rather than stolen, you begin to see your life differently. You stop asking, “Who took this from me?” And start asking, “Where did I begin to defer what I should have governed?” if you can see where authority was set down, you can return to that place.

Authority is rarely lost in a single moment. It is laid down slowly, quietly, almost politely. And that is why so many people do not realize it is happening until they feel the cold. But once you recognize the pattern, you also recognize something hopeful: What was set down can be picked up again. You simply have to remember where you left it.

UNGOVERNED HUNGER AND BURNING THE PASSPORT

Appetite vs access – Short-term relief, long-term loss. There is a particular kind of mistake people make when they are under pressure. They use what grants them access to try to solve what requires provision. This is desperation born from misalignment.

Imagine someone using a passport to patch a shoe, or to plug a hole in a roof. Or to burn for warmth. A passport is not warmth, it is not insulation; It is not patch material; It is **authorization**. Sadly, in moments of urgency, a person may destroy the very thing that allows them to leave their situation later, simply to survive it now.

That is what Scripture shows again and again.

Esau trades his birthright for stew. Judas trades loyalty for silver. Adam reaches for fruit. People exchange long-term authority for short-term relief, because they are hungry. Hungry for comfort. Hungry for relief. Hungry for approval. Hungry for immediate resolution. That is lustful appetite and ungoverned hunger.

Authority does not feel like food. It does not feel like shelter. It does not feel like relief. Authority is the currency of food, shelter, peace, joy, safety and protection, deliverance and freedom, in the spirit realm. Authority feels abstract until the moment you need access. If this is not known, people consume what was meant to grant passage in order to solve what feels urgent in the moment.

They burn the passport to stay warm. And later, they wonder why they cannot leave that place they got trapped into or stuck in looking for something for their appetite. Like a mouse looking at cheese in a trap. Except the person doesn't see the trap, just the cheese and they would never for a moment think they are a rodent or could be trapped.

This is why appetite is so dangerous when it is not governed. Appetite always demands *now*. Authority always operates in *order*. Appetite says, "Fix this." Authority says, "Steward this." Appetite wants relief. Authority protects access. Many people have not lost authority because they were reckless. They lost it because they were trying to survive. They were solving immediate problems with the wrong tools. They were solving immediate problems with expensive eternal tools. They were solving natural problems with *spiritual* tools. Spiritual tools are generational and they shouldn't be spent on a taco on Tuesday.

Just as natural solutions cannot solve spiritual problems, spiritual tools are far too precious to be used today on natural, perishable things. They used what was meant for stewardship to satisfy hunger. The tragedy is that they did not realize what they were holding at the time. It's like holding seeds in your hands but you don't plant them; you eat them. Now what will get you out of hunger in the next season, or even the next day?

This is why so many people say, years later "I wish I had known." They are not wishing they had been stronger. They are wishing they had recognized the value of what they were about to trade. Authority was never meant to be consumed to solve survival. It was meant to grant access beyond survival.

That is the difference. When you understand this, you stop judging your past through the lens of stupidity and begin seeing it through the lens of ungoverned hunger. Once you see this pattern, you begin to recognize it in small decisions as well. Every time you sacrifice long-term peace for short-term relief… Every time you blur a boundary to avoid discomfort, every time you trade discernment for approval… You are burning something that was meant to carry you further. The good news is that authority, because it is entrusted and not owned, can be restored.

But restoration requires recognizing what was consumed. You cannot protect what you do not know you are holding. You will stop burning passports once you understand what they are for. Ungoverned hunger does not make you a bad person. It makes you a person who did not recognize the value of what was in your hands.

Once you recognize it, something changes. You begin to protect access instead of chasing relief. You begin to steward what you once consumed. And authority begins to return to its proper place.

A passport is not warmth. It is not insulation. It is not patch material. It is authorization. And yet man repeatedly uses what grants access to try to solve what requires provision. That is the tragedy. When a person misuses and loses a passport, they are not being innovative. They are being desperate and misaligned. They may be solving an immediate need but destroying a long-term authority.

Scripture shows this pattern again and again: Esau burns his passport for stew. Judas trades his passport for silver. Adam spends his passport on fruit. Jezebel's prophets rent theirs for food. None of them did that because they lacked value, but because they lacked discernment of what they were holding.

Authority does not feel like food. It does not feel like shelter. It does not feel like relief. Authority feels abstract until the moment access is required. The carnal man is most often only concerned with things he can see in the natural. So, people sacrifice future passage to survive present pressure. That is not so much stupidity as it is ungoverned hunger.

Authority was never meant to be consumed to solve survival, it was meant to grant access beyond it. If we lose the authority to get out of places—well, ideally to never land in bad situations and places, then we will ever wonder why we cannot leave when we need to get out. We may wonder why things aren't working for us. We may wonder how come I'm speaking to this mountain, but it is not moving, it is not obeying?

There is hope; what was given can be re-governed. God forgives and you may be restored into your rightful authority again.

You are not a joke. You are not trivial. You are important to God and there is an exceeding weight to the Glory He has given each of us. If you stepped out from under authority, you lost it. And you were holding something that mattered.

A person can relinquish authority without realizing the exact moment, method, or recipient. Not because authority is fragile — but because authority is often surrendered incrementally, not ceremonially.

Authority is often relinquished (Biblically speaking) Rarely does Scripture show people standing up and saying, I now give my authority away." Instead, it looks like this: one decision under pressure, one compromise for relief, one silence to avoid conflict, one appetite prioritized over discernment, or possibly one boundary blurred -- "just this time, to get it out of my system."

Authority is laid down, not ripped away. That's why many people can say truthfully: "I don't know when things changed — I just know they did."

People don't know where it went because authority is not an object — it's relational and functional. You don't "hand it over" like keys. You defer it to fear, or maybe to approval, to appetite, to provision, to comfort, or maybe for what you think is survival. Whatever you defer to begins to decide for you. That's governance transfer.

The Bible consistently treats loss of authority as something that happens through neglect, misplaced trust, prolonged compromise, abdication rather than rebellion Which is why restoration is possible. If authority were stolen, recovery would require force. Because it was yielded, recovery requires recognition and return. This means People are not always "rebellious." They are often unaware. And ignorance does not mean permanence.

Authority can be reclaimed, re-aligned, and re-governed. But only after it is recognized as lost. Authority is most often lost not through defiance, but through unrecognized surrender like a coat left behind in childhood, authority can be misplaced without knowing when — until the cold reveals it.

A person can relinquish authority without realizing the exact moment, method, or recipient. Not because authority is fragile — but because authority is often surrendered incrementally, not ceremonially, *unintentionally*.

RELIGIOUS AUTHORITY GONE WRONG

As Christians we are in relationship with God as Father. We are in Christ; we are under Divine Authority. That is the original placement and purpose of man having been created. Even though Adam and Eve fell, Jesus bought us back, so we are restored to dominion and we have authority. As we visit and especially join the church of our choice we are now set under the authority of the pastor or leader of that congregation and that person should also be under Christ. However, if they are not, then there will be an erosion of authority from the members of that local Body.

When rituals replace relationship with God, authority will be lost. When there are so many rules—when a person joins the 'church' rather than getting saved and beginning a relationship with God as Father, authority will not be made available to that member. That is called legalism. It is counterfeit order and there will be no access to the authority of God, whether that Christian knows if the ministry is counterfeit or not.

Religious authority can go profoundly wrong when manipulation disguised as submission, alongside Spiritual theatrics and fear-based control systems. Fear replaces order. People are afraid not to comply for many reasons, spiritual, social, emotional—they don't want to lose their position in the church. This is coercion authority, not Biblical alignment.

When there is learning without governance, as when Judas showed his true colors by calling Jesus, Rabbi and not Lord. People may be taught, correct, or instructed while never being required to exercise true governance themselves. There may be compliance, but not transformation.

You can't fake authority. You can't fake alignment. True authority flows through alignment, not by pressure, or theatrics. Some people may appear submissive but in reality, are they? Only God knows their heart, so I'm not judging anyone, but by their fruit we shall know them. Are they set under authority. Can they speak to the fig tree as Jesus did? Will the storm stop at their command? Will their prayers, decrees, declarations, cries and commands be heard and obeyed. God decides that, but with our own eyes we can see if their fruit is good and that it remains.

And, they can see us, too.

True submission aligns a person with God's order and strengthens their capacity to govern their own life. Manipulative submission weakens the man—his self-governance, replaces Peace with fear, and substitutes control for stewardship.

FOUNDATIONS YOU DID NOT CHOOSE

At some point in understanding authority, a difficult realization appears: Not all of the foundations you stand on were poured by you.

Some were laid long before you had a voice. Some were shaped by decisions you did not make. Some were formed by environments you did not choose.

yet, you are standing on them. This is where many people feel stuck. They recognize that something in their life feels unstable, but they also recognize: *"I didn't build this."*

That tension is real.

Scripture does not ignore generational impact. Patterns travel through families. Fears are learned. Beliefs are inherited. Ways of responding to pressure are modeled long before they are examined. These things become part of the foundation a person grows up on. Not because they chose it. Because it was there.

This is where authority and forgiveness meet.

Because even though you did not choose the foundation, you are now responsible for what you build on it.

That is not unfair. It is simply reality. You cannot change what was poured. But you can decide what you build next. Forgiveness becomes essential here, not as emotion, but as jurisdiction.

Unforgiveness ties you to foundations you did not choose. It keeps you anchored to what harmed you. It keeps you building in reaction instead of intention. Forgiveness does something powerful: It releases your future from the claims of the past. Forgiveness is not saying: "It didn't matter." "It wasn't wrong." "I deserved it."

Forgiveness is saying **"This will no longer govern what I build."** That is jurisdiction. Many people try to repair their lives while still holding anger toward the foundations they inherited. But you cannot lay new structure while holding unresolved claims against the old one. The old foundation keeps pulling your attention backward.

Forgiveness severs that pull.

This is why foundation work is impossible without forgiveness. Because foundation work exposes things that were decided for you emotional patterns. relational habits. responses to stress. beliefs about yourself and others. You begin to see that some of what you must repair, you did not create.

And that realization can easily turn into resentment. But resentment is not strength. It is continued submission to what already weakened you. Forgiveness is where authority quietly returns.

Because you are no longer reacting. You are choosing. You are no longer compensating. You are building. You are no longer tied to what was. You are responsible for what will be. Scripture holds this truth gently but clearly. Generational consequences are real. But generational cycles are not permanent.

You are not responsible for what was poured. But you are responsible for what you construct. This realization is not heavy. It is freeing. Your authority does not begin with the foundations you inherited. It begins with the ones you choose to lay. Forgiveness is what allows you to begin.

HE FIRST DESCENDED

(Descent Before Ascent)

There is a pattern in Scripture that is easy to overlook but impossible to ignore once seen: Before ascent, there is descent. Before elevation, there is lowering. Before restoration, there is return to foundation.

He who descended is the One who also ascended…
(Ephesians 4)

This is not only about Christ. It is a pattern for how authority is lawfully restored in man. Many people want authority back without revisiting the place where it weakened. They want Peace without examining the leak. They want clarity without revisiting confusion. They want strength without returning to the foundation.

But authority cannot be rebuilt from the top down. It must be rebuilt from the bottom up. This is why restoration often feels like going backward. You find yourself addressing things you thought were long settled. You revisit patterns you hoped were gone. You face memories, habits, and decisions that feel small but carry weight. It can feel discouraging. But this is not regression. It is descent. And descent is lawful.

Foundation work cannot be skipped because authority rests on what you stand on, not what you reach for.

You cannot place new weight on old cracks. You cannot build upward while ignoring what lies beneath. If you try, the same instability will reappear later, often with greater consequence.

This is why people sometimes avoid praying for "foundation work." They sense that it will be uncomfortable. They sense it will uncover things. They sense it will require honesty they would rather avoid. But foundation work is not punishment. It is Mercy. Because it allows you to repair quietly what would otherwise collapse publicly. Descent is where you forgive what still has influence. correct what still has effect. confront what still has weight. rebuild what still bears load.

This is slow work, but it is permanent work.

Authority that is rebuilt from descent does not wobble when pressure comes. Because it has been re-rooted. Because it has been re-examined. Because it is no longer resting on what you hoped was strong, but on what you know has been repaired.

This is why Scripture never rushes restoration. It allows time for descent. Because ascent without descent produces fragile authority — impressive for a moment, unstable over time. When you understand this, you stop resisting the return to foundational matters. You begin to see it as a necessary part of authority being restored, not a sign that something is wrong.

You are not going backward.

You are going down so that you can rise without fear of collapse. He first descended. And because of that, His ascent was unshakeable. The same pattern holds true for man. Authority that rises without descent is loud. Authority that rises after descent is steady, and steady authority is what endures.

RECOGNITION, RETURN, AND RE-ALIGNMENT

When authority has been weakened, the natural instinct is to try to get it back through effort. People try to be stronger. More disciplined. More vocal. More determined. But authority is not restored through force. It is restored through recognition and return.

The first step in restoration is not action. It is recognition. You begin to see where authority was laid down. Where governance weakened. Where alignment shifted. This is not a moment of shame.

It is a moment of clarity. Because once you can see it, you can return from it. The prodigal son did not fight his way back into his father's house. He recognized where he was. He returned. He realigned himself with the place he belonged. Authority met him there.

It did not require force. It required return. This is why restoration is relational. Authority flows through alignment with God's order, not through personal effort. You do not manufacture authority by trying harder. You step back into the structure where authority already flows.

Many people exhaust themselves trying to regain what they lost by pushing harder in the same direction that led them away. They try to speak louder. Decide faster. Control more. But force never works because authority was never about control.

It was about order. Re-alignment is quiet.

It looks like returning to small acts of governance, restoring boundaries, practicing restraint, choosing obedience in simple areas. These actions may feel insignificant, but they re-position you within the flow of authority. Once you are re-positioned, authority begins to function again, without strain.

This is why restoration often feels surprisingly gentle. You expect difficulty. You expect resistance. But what you find is that authority has been waiting for you to come back into place. It was not hiding. It was not lost. You were simply out of alignment.

Recognition leads to return. Return leads to re-alignment. Re-alignment allows authority to operate again. That is the pattern. You do not reclaim authority by force. You reclaim it by standing again where you belong. As you do, authority meets you there as if it had never left. In truth, it hadn't; you had simply stepped outside of its flow.

FAITHFUL IN LITTLE: AUTHORITY RE-CONFIRMED

When authority begins to return, many people expect it to look dramatic. They expect sudden confidence, sudden influence. They believe they will see a sudden change that everyone can see. But restoration does not begin publicly. It begins quietly, in small places that no one else notices.

He who is faithful in little is faithful also in much...
(Luke 16)

This is not a lesson about reward. It is a lesson about confirmation. Authority is re-confirmed in the small before it is trusted in the visible. After recognition, return, and re-alignment, life does not immediately expand.

Instead, you find yourself facing ordinary decisions, governing your words. honoring your boundaries. choosing restraint. showing up consistently. doing what is right when no one is watching.

These things may feel unrelated to authority. But they are where authority is re-established. This is where many people grow impatient. They feel ready for more. They feel restored. They want to step forward again.

But authority does not move at the speed of desire.

It moves at the speed of proven steadiness. Restoration is progressive because governance must become natural again. Not forced. Not performed.

Authority that returns too quickly can rest on habits that are not yet stable. So, Scripture allows time for faithfulness to settle into daily life. This is why public authority comes last. Not because it is unimportant. But because it is visible. And what is visible must be supported by what is already secure. If public authority returns before private governance is steady, collapse will follow.

When private governance is consistent, public authority rests lightly and naturally. This is also where peace begins to return. You stop trying to prove that you have changed. You simply live differently. You stop trying to demonstrate authority. You simply carry it. Faithfulness in little things is where authority is re-confirmed, not just restored. Restoration says, "You are back in place." Re-confirmation says, "You can be trusted here again." That trust is built quietly.

Over time, you notice something subtle. Decisions feel lighter. Confidence feels calmer. Your words carry weight again without effort. This is not because you are trying harder. It is because authority has been rebuilt from the foundation upward. Authority that is re-confirmed through faithfulness is not fragile. It does not depend on mood, performance, or recognition.

It rests on a life that has learned again how to govern small things well. From there, everything else can safely grow.

THE TYPES OF AUTHORITY MAN STEWARDS

SELF-GOVERNANCE AUTHORITY

Before a person can steward anything outside of themselves, they must learn to govern what is within themselves. This is the most overlooked form of authority because it is invisible.

No one sees it. No one applauds it. No one rewards it publicly. But every other form of authority rests on it. Self-governance authority is the ability to rule appetite, speech, emotion, impulse, reaction, or desire. This is not about personality; it is about restraint.

It is about choosing what you will allow to direct you and what you will not. This is why Scripture pays such close attention to small things such as guarding the tongue, patience under pressure, obedience in quiet moments, resisting temptation, honoring boundaries.

These do not appear impressive, but they are foundational. Because a person who cannot govern themselves cannot safely govern anything else.

This is where authority first weakened in the Garden at Eden. This was not about ruling the Earth, but in ruling appetite. A single decision to satisfy desire over order disrupted everything. That is how powerful self-governance is.

This is also why many people feel unstable in other areas of life without realizing the root issue. They may struggle in relationships. In work. In peace of mind.

But often, the earliest crack is in self-governance. They allow appetite, emotion, or impulse to make decisions that should have been governed. Over time, the effects spread. Self-governance is not harsh. It is protective. It keeps you from trading long-term authority for short-term relief. It keeps you from speaking words you must later repair. It keeps you from making decisions you must later undo. It keeps your life steady.

He that hath no rule over his own spirit is like a city that is broken down, and without walls. (Proverbs 25:28)

This is why self-governance stabilizes all other forms of authority. Because you carry yourself into every situation. You carry your habits into your relationships. You carry your impulses into your work. You carry your discipline into your decisions.

There is no separation. It's like that saying, *Everywhere you go, there you are.*

When self-governance is strong, other forms of authority feel lighter. When it is weak, everything feels heavier than it should. That is not coincidence. That is structure. This is also where restoration must always begin. It starts with small, quiet choices that no one else sees. Because self-governance is where authority becomes trustworthy again.

You may never receive recognition for self-governance. But you will feel the difference everywhere. Peace becomes easier to hold. Clarity becomes easier to maintain. Decisions become easier to make. Because you are no longer at the mercy of what you feel in the moment. You are governing yourself, which is the first, strongest form of authority a person can possess.

RELATIONAL AUTHORITY

Once a person learns to govern themselves, authority naturally begins to express itself in relationships. This is where authority becomes visible in daily life. Not through position. Not through titles. But through how a person stands in covenant with others.

Relational authority includes marriage, family, close bonds, and covenant commitments. These are not casual connections. They are places where authority is shared, tested, and strengthened. Because relationships require stewardship beyond the self.

This is why disorder in relationships affects everything else. When relational authority weakens peace becomes harder to maintain, decisions become heavier, clarity becomes clouded, emotional stability wavers. Not because relationships are emotional. Because they are structural.

They are part of the authority system a person stands in. Marriage, in particular, is not simply companionship; it is covenant authority.

Two people agreeing to stand in shared governance of life requires boundaries, self-governance, forgiveness, and alignment. Without these, marriage becomes strain instead of support. Family operates similarly. The way authority is handled within a family shapes how individuals learn to handle authority everywhere else.

If authority is abused, neglected, or misunderstood at home, it often creates confusion that follows a person into adulthood. Because relational authority is often where we first learn what authority looks like. This is why Scripture places such importance on how people behave within their households. Not because home life is private. But because it is foundational.

If authority cannot function here, it will struggle to function elsewhere. Relational authority requires more than feelings. It requires covenant thinking. It requires recognizing that what you do affects not only you, but those joined to you. That awareness is part of authority. When relational authority is healthy, everything else feels steadier.

A person thinks more clearly. Speaks more carefully. Acts more thoughtfully. Because they are aware that they are not standing alone. When relational authority is fractured, everything feels heavier. Because a person is trying to carry life alone when it was designed to be shared.

That strain shows up everywhere.

This is why repairing relational authority is often part of restoring overall authority. Not because relationships are sentimental, financially advantageous, or fun, but because they are structural. They are part of how authority was designed to operate in man's life.

Relational authority is where self-governance is tested and refined. It is where forgiveness becomes necessary. Where boundaries must be respected. Where alignment must be practiced daily. When it is strong, it stabilizes everything around it. Because a person is no longer standing alone. They are standing in covenant which is one of the strongest expressions of authority that Scripture reveals.

VOCATIONAL / ASSIGNMENT AUTHORITY

Not all authority in a person's life is permanent. Some authority is tied to **assignment**. This includes roles, offices, responsibilities, positions of trust, seasons of work and service.

This is vocational authority. Vocational authority is the authority you carry because of what you have been entrusted to do, not simply who you are. A judge carries authority in the courtroom. A teacher carries authority in the classroom. A parent carries authority in the home. A leader carries authority within their sphere of responsibility.

This authority is real. But it is **assignment-based**. This is where many people struggle. They confuse assignment authority with personal authority. So, when a role ends, they feel as if something in them has ended. But what has ended is the assignment, not the person.

Scripture shows this clearly.

Kings reign for a season.
Prophets speak for a time.
Leaders rise and step down.

The authority attached to the role ends when the assignment ends. But the person remains entrusted in other areas. This is why seasons of transition feel unsettling. A person may no longer carry the authority they once had in a specific role, and they mistake that for loss of worth. But authority tied to assignment is meant to be temporary.

It is not meant to define identity.

Understanding this prevents two common mistakes. First, clinging to roles that have ended. People try to hold onto positions long after the assignment has passed, because they fear losing authority. Second, feeling diminished when seasons change.

People think they have lost something essential, when in reality, they have simply completed an assignment. Vocational authority is important, but it is not ultimate. It is one layer in the larger structure of authority in a person's life.

When you understand this, you begin to see roles and responsibilities as trusts for a time, not possessions to keep. This also explains why authority sometimes shifts throughout life. New assignments bring new forms of authority. Old assignments release old forms of authority.

This is not instability. It is movement. When a person knows who they are, and stands securely in relational authority and self-governance, vocational changes do not shake them.

They understand that what they carry in an assignment is real, but temporary. They release it when the time comes without fear. Vocational authority teaches humility. Because you learn that authority is something you hold for a purpose, not something you own.

When the purpose is complete, you lay it down--, not as loss, but as completion. Authority that is tied to assignment ends when the assignment ends. Understanding that allows you to move through seasons of life with steadiness instead of fear, because you know that what you are entrusted with next will meet you in the next place you are called to stand.

CIVIC AND SOCIAL AUTHORITY

Beyond the authority of the self, relationships, and personal assignments, there is another layer that affects every person Civic and social authority This includes governments, laws, institutions, social structures, recognized positions of order. These are not personal. They are structural. And they exist whether you approve of them or not.

Scripture speaks clearly about this:

There is no authority except from God, and those that exist have been instituted... (Romans 13)

This does not mean every authority is righteous. It means every authority is recognized within God's order. Civic authority is authority that must be **acknowledged**, even when it is not **approved**. You may disagree with it. You may dislike it. You may resist aspects of it. But you cannot pretend it does not exist. This is where many people lose clarity. They assume that if they do not approve of an authority, they are free to ignore it. But authority does not disappear because of disagreement.

It remains structurally present. And wise people learn how to live within that reality without losing their own governance. This is why Scripture shows examples of people navigating civic authority carefully.

Joseph in Egypt.
Daniel in Babylon.
Paul under Roman rule.

They did not collapse under civic authority, nor did they pretend it did not exist. They understood how to live within it without surrendering their own alignment. Civic authority teaches something important:

Authority is bigger than personal preference. It reminds you that you live within a structure larger than yourself. And learning how to stand properly within that structure is part of understanding authority in your own life. This also explains why chaos in society often creates instability in individuals. When civic authority weakens or becomes confused, people feel it.

They don't feel it because they are directly involved, but because the structure around them has shifted. Structure affects everyone. Understanding civic authority helps you avoid two extremes, the first is blind submission without discernment. The second is rebellion without Wisdom.

Civic authority teaches you how to recognize authority without losing yourself. Authority acknowledged is different from authority approved.

You may not approve of a structure, but you still recognize its place in the order of things. And that recognition allows you to move wisely instead of reactively.

Civic and social authority are reminders that authority is not only personal and relational. It is also structural and communal. Learning to navigate that wisely is part of being a person who understands how authority truly functions.

SPIRITUAL AUTHORITY

Spiritual authority is often the most misunderstood form of authority because it is the least visible and the easiest to imitate. People assume spiritual authority is loud. They assume it is dramatic. They assume it is measured by intensity, emotion, or volume. Scripture presents it very differently. Spiritual authority is quiet, steady, and deeply connected to alignment. Spiritual authority operates through the Word, the Name, command,

But none of these function properly outside of order. You can speak loudly and have no authority. You can speak calmly and have great authority. Because spiritual authority does not respond to volume. It responds to alignment. Jesus did not strain to exercise spiritual authority. He did not shout. He did not perform. He spoke, and things responded. Not because He was forceful, but because He was perfectly aligned.

This is why the sons of Sceva in Scripture could say the right words and see no result. They used the language of authority without standing in the alignment that makes authority function. Spiritual authority cannot be borrowed. It cannot be imitated. It cannot be forced.

It flows from order.

The Word carries authority because it originates in God's order. The Name carries authority because it represents alignment with God's rule. Command carries authority when it is spoken from a life that is properly positioned under that order.

Without alignment, these become empty forms. This is why spiritual authority is connected to everything you have already read. Self-governance. Relational authority. Vocational steadiness. Civic awareness.

All of these contribute to the alignment that allows spiritual authority to function naturally. Many people exhaust themselves trying to exercise spiritual authority while ignoring the foundations that support it. They try to command outcomes without addressing the areas where their own governance is weak.

But spiritual authority is not a tool to compensate for disorder. It is an expression of order. When alignment is present, spiritual authority is calm. You do not feel the need to prove anything. You do not feel the need to be loud. You simply speak, and what needs to respond, responds.

This is why alignment matters more than volume. Because authority in the spiritual realm recognizes order, not noise. It responds to position, not performance. Spiritual authority is not something you acquire. It is something that becomes evident when you are standing correctly.

when you are, you do not need to force it. It flows through you as naturally as the other forms of authority you steward. Quiet. Steady. Unmistakable.

For clarity: Authority is not anointing; they are different things. **Authority** is delegated jurisdiction, legitimate standing, lawful right to operate within a sphere. Authority answers question such as, "By what right?"

Authority is structural, positional, and accountable. Marriage authority, for example, and which we will discuss in the next chapter, exists because covenant creates jurisdiction. You do not have marital authority before you are married — because you are not in that covenant structure yet.

Anointing is empowerment. It is Grace for function. It is divine enablement. Anointing answers, "With what empowerment?" Anointing is capacity from God to function in a role.

You can have authority without strong visible anointing. You can have anointing without proper authority. Ideally, they align.

One of my friends says, "No one gets the anointing to be married until they get married." There is Grace for a role that becomes active once the role exists. Just as there is a parenting Grace that shows up when you become a parent. Pastoral Grace activates when you step into pastoral office, and so on. That's not authority. That's enablement. That's anointing.

A man can have natural authority and not be recognized as a man of authority in the spirit. You want God's Authority. Divine Authority foremost; the rest will follow. When a man has the favor of God, he will also have the favor of man. Having natural authority does not mean you have *arrived* in the spirit. You can have a title, a platform, a following, money, influence, education, rank, or any combination of those things, and still lack spiritual authority.

Natural authority is granted by systems. Spiritual authority is recognized by realms. In Scripture, the sons of Sceva had religious proximity. But when they tried to exercise authority, the demon said: "Jesus I know. Paul I recognize. But who are you?" That was about legitimacy. Spiritual authority is not assumed; it is aligned.

Jesus had both natural and spiritual authority; His spiritual authority flowed from alignment with the Father. "I do nothing except what I see My Father doing." That's why storms obeyed. That's why demons obeyed. Because Heaven affirmed Him.

Recognition in the Spirit means you are spiritually legit. You are aligned with God's governance. When you are aligned: faithful, diligent, trustworthy. You are ordered, governed, submitted to God; that is spiritual legitimacy.

Recognition in the spirit does not mean: Demons know your name or that you feel powerful.

And the seventy returned
again with joy, saying, Lord, even the devils are
subject unto us through thy name (Luke 10:17)

Notwithstanding in this rejoice not, that the spirits are
subject unto
you; but rather rejoice, because your names are
written in heaven. (Luke 10:20)

Having your name <u>written</u> means you are aligned. If God recognizes you, then the spirit realm must. Jesus said: "Seek first the Kingdom… and all these things will be added." Don't chase things, status, wealth, marriage. You **<u>align</u>**, then, what is appropriate is added. Actually, it will chase you. If you have to chase it, you will most likely need violence to keep it.

WHEN HE WRITES YOUR NAME DOWN; HE KNOWS YOU. This is unlike those whom He told to get away from Him because He never knew them. This means some things can be attained by violence and corruption, but they won't remain.

Many will say to me in that day, Lord, Lord, have
we not prophesied in thy name? and in thy name have
cast out devils? and in thy name done many wonderful
works? … I never knew you: depart from me, ye
that work iniquity. (Matthew 7:22-23)

AUTHORITY OVER MARRIAGE: WHY DESIRE IS NOT ENOUGH

WHEN AUTHORITY IS DESIRED BUT ELUSIVE

Few desires are as strong, sincere, and widespread as the desire to be married. And yet, for many people, marriage feels elusive, delayed, complicated, or fragile. This often leads to questions such as: *What am I doing wrong? Why does this seem easy for others and difficult for me? Is something being withheld from me?*

These questions are painful because they assume that desire should be enough. But marriage is not governed by desire. It is governed by covenant authority. From the beginning, marriage is introduced not as romance, but as order.

It is not good that the man should be alone (Genesis 2)

This is not about loneliness; it is about structure. Marriage is a joining of two lives into shared governance. That requires more than longing. It requires readiness to steward covenant.

Covenant authority is different from relational desire. Desire says, "I want to be with you." Covenant says, "I am prepared to stand with you in order, responsibility, and restraint." That is a different level of maturity.

This is why marriage responds to order, not longing. A person may deeply desire marriage and yet still be strengthening the layers of authority that make covenant safe. This is not punishment; it is protection.

Marriage is weight-bearing. If entered without the proper foundations, it becomes strain instead of support. This is also why many relationships begin with excitement and end with confusion. The desire was present. The covenant authority was not yet ready. So, what began as connection became instability.

Marriage requires self-governance, boundaries, forgiveness, alignment under God's order, the ability to share authority without control. These are not romantic qualities; they are structural ones. Without them, marriage feels heavy instead of steady. This is why some people find marriage later in life, after they have learned to stand well alone.

Marriage is not a solution to instability; it is a structure that depends on stability. Understanding this removes shame. Not being married does not mean you are overlooked. It may mean you are being prepared to carry something that requires order. It may mean that foundations are being strengthened behind the scenes.

Marriage is not a prize for longing; it is a trust given where covenant authority can be sustained. When it comes in order, it does not feel fragile, it feels steady.

Authority over marriage is not about finding the right person first. It is about becoming a person who can stand in covenant safely. When two such people meet, marriage does not strain them; it supports them.

Marriage responds to **order**. When that order is present, desire finds its rightful place within covenant, not the other way around.

How do I get my marriage authority back? This might be the question of the year. Well, I cannot promise, "Here's how to get your spouse back in line." But I can offer how to re-enter rightful covenant alignment. We can talk about that. **First,** authority in marriage is not dominance. Marriage authority is not about control or winning arguments. Marriage is covenant alignment under God. The question is not about how to fix your spouse. But you should ask: "Where did alignment fracture?"

Second: Marriage authority is restored the same way all authority is, through Recognition. Return. Realignment.

So, the steps are as before:

1. Self-governance first.
    - Repent where needed
    - Remove defensiveness.
    - Stop spiritualizing dysfunction.
    - Restore integrity in speech and behavior.

2. **Re-establish covenant posture.**
    - Recommit to faithfulness.
    - Reinforce exclusivity.
    - Remove third-party loyalties (emotional or otherwise).
3. **Restore boundaries.**
    - No manipulation.
    - No emotional leverage.
    - No power plays.
4. **Return to daily alignment.**
    - Pray together (if possible).
    - Speak life, not accusation.
    - Rebuild trust slowly.

Authority is not seized; it is re-earned through faithful governance.

Third: If the Other Person Is Not Aligning - Marriage authority is mutual covenant. You cannot unilaterally restore full relational authority if the other party refuses covenant. You can restore your alignment.You cannot force theirs; worry 'bout yourself.

Authority is never regained through force. It is reestablished through faithful structure. Sometimes that leads to healing. Sometimes it leads to clarity, but never control.

Marriage authority is not reclaimed by assertion but by alignment. It returns when covenant is honored again. You cannot demand covenant authority. You must stand in covenant integrity until authority recognizes alignment.

- "Have I lost something?"
- "Did I *forfeit* marital authority?"
- "Is marriage not responding to me because of misalignment?"
- "Did I trade something?"

First truth to anchor marriage is not dispensed as a prize for moral perfection. It is covenant alignment between two willing persons under God. Marital authority is not something you possess in advance. It is something you step into when covenant is formed.

Before covenant, what you govern is:

- your self-governance
- your appetite
- your boundaries
- your alignment

You cannot “get marriage authority back” if you are not currently in covenant. You can only ensure you are governable within covenant when it forms.

If you think: “I sinned. I lost marital authority.” Please know this: **Sin does not permanently erase covenant eligibility.** misalignment does distort readiness. So, the path forward is not “Recover a marital badge, it is:

- Restore self-governance.
- Repair covenant integrity in current relationships.
- Remove appetite-driven patterns.
- Stand in alignment consistently.

Marriage responds to alignment — not desperation. Marriage is not drawn by longing. It is sustained by governance.

Now, about those already married who may feel they “lost their unmarried authority”—maybe they feel diminished, overruled, ignored, erased-- .that’s usually self-governance leakage, not loss of covenant authority. They need restoration of personal alignment, not escape from marriage.

Married or unmarried: Authority is not recovered by force. It is recognized when alignment returns. You are not locked out of covenant by past failure, unless you refuse to repent. But covenant requires present governance.

Work out your own salvation with fear and trembling.
(Philippians 2:12)

Marriage will absolutely expose impatience, pride, selfishness, tone, control tendencies, forgiveness gaps, boundary confusion, and ego. It's a sanctification accelerator.

Though powerful, marriage is not the only crucible.

Singleness also refines, but differently. Solitude, self-governance without witness, contentment, discipline without external accountability all will be challenged in life, married or single. Marriage refines relationally. Singleness refines internally. Both work salvation out — just differently. If you want to see how much governance you actually have, get married. Marriage doesn't create sanctification — it accelerates it. Relational authority is where self-governance is tested.

If it seems that you can't find your person or get married, **sexual rights is more the issue than marital authority.**

SEXUAL RIGHTS IS ABOUT AUTHORITY

In Scripture, rights are never about indulgence. They are about jurisdiction. So, when a pastor speaks about *sexual rights*, they are really talking about: Who has lawful authority over sexual access, expression, and stewardship — and when. That places sexuality squarely inside the frameworks of authority.

Where this shows up, Biblically, Paul uses explicit authority language, not permission language, in 1 Corinthians 7:

> The wife does not have authority over her own body, but the husband does. Likewise the husband does not have authority over his own body, but the wife does.

That is not romantic language. That is jurisdictional language.

It tells us three things at once. Sexuality is governed, not autonomous. Authority over sexuality can be shared by covenant. Rights exist within order, not outside it. Sexual rights are an *authority issue*, not a desire issue.

Sexuality is a domain of authority. Sexuality involves access, consent, restraint, timing, covenant, and stewardship of life. Those are all authority categories. Which means sexuality cannot be understood correctly without understanding self-governance, relational authority, covenant authority, boundaries. That's why so much confusion exists around sex — because people treat it as appetite when it is actually jurisdiction.

"Sexual rights" can sound modern or political, which makes people nervous. Biblically, *rights* means what is lawful, what is permitted, what is authorized, what is protected. A good teacher uses that term not to encourage indulgence, but to limit misuse. Because when rights are undefined, abuse fills the gap.

Sexual authority sits at the intersection of self-governance (can I restrain appetite?). relational authority (am I joined in covenant?). assignment authority (what season am I in?). spiritual authority (am I aligned or compensating?). Ungoverned sexuality is one of the fastest ways authority leaks — which is exactly why *ungoverned hunger* leads naturally to *authority* issues and loss of authority.

Sexuality is not governed by desire, but by authority. Where authority is unclear, confusion and misuse follow. Sexual rights exist only where sexual authority is properly ordered.

Observing sexual rights means you are not entitled to access without covenant. You are not permitted to violate yourself or others. There are strict laws in the Old Testament as well as in in our own modern government. You are not free to consume what you are meant to steward. Violations of sexual rights is used for rituals, trauma and to cause the loss of authority. In civil society those under a certain age cannot even give consent; it is not theirs to give. Their father is custodian of sexual rights until a child is of the age of consent. On deliverance ground, it is known as a method of exchange, trade and theft of virtues.

Authority governs appetite. Sex is appetite. Therefore, sex must be governed by authority. Unauthorized use is a direct child of *Authority* and *Ungoverned Hunger*. There is an owner. There are terms of use. Access is conditional. Violation produces consequence, not neutrality. That is jurisdiction.

Sexuality is one of the most commonly mis-jurisdictioned domains in human life.

Marriage is not blocked by longing, It is blocked by jurisdictional disorder. When sexual access is premature, misaligned, compensatory, ungoverned. It trains the soul to bypass covenant structure. Then people wonder why covenant won't settle.

Unauthorized use is not rebellion, it is appetite acting as permission. When desire replaces authorization, access becomes violation, even when both parties agree. Most are not married, or can't even seem to meet their right person.... *"Why does this one thing feel blocked when I desire it so deeply?"*

Most teachings either spiritualize it away ("just wait"), psychologize it ("work on yourself"), or romanticize it ("love will find you").

I am endeavoring to explain it to you structurally.

Marriage is not scarce; it is ordered. So many sincere, faithful, intelligent people are emotionally ready, are spiritually hungry, are relationally kind. …and still can't seem to cross that threshold. Not because they are defective. But because **authority precedes access** — and no one ever taught them that.

Marriage responds to order, not longing. You might be saying any of the following: *"Authority was never explained." "Order was never taught." "Desire was mistaken for permission."* You weren't rejected — you were unprepared for something weight-bearing. Could be why the boring librarian has a spouse and others don't; the librarian didn't lose her marriage authority in high school.

Marriage is one of the clearest places where authority, covenant, self-governance, restraint, and alignment all converge. If authority is misunderstood here, the consequences are personal and long-lasting — which is why the confusion is so painful.

God is not withholding spouses; He is protecting covenant. *Sometimes* covenant protection often looks like delay to the person experiencing it. Delay is not absence, it's guarded access.

Marriage is also sacred and those who play with it as if it a plaything do not get out of it what they should and they don't fulfill their (sacred) reason for being in it. They just want the fun part; and it can be fun, but that's not all it is. It is a covenant. How many covenants in the Bible were made "for fun"? None. Zero. Not one.

Marriage is sacred, which means it is set apart for purpose, not for entertainment. Fun may exist *inside* covenant — but covenant is never created *for* fun.

Every covenant in Scripture was made because something serious, weight-bearing, and generational was at stake.

Covenants were made for preservation, order, legacy, governance, redemption, and alignment with God. Never for amusement. Never for novelty. Never for pleasure-first reasons. Pleasure may follow covenant — but it never precedes it.

What happens when covenant is treated like a toy? What happens when people approach marriage primarily for companionship without responsibility, intimacy without governance, benefit without sacrifice, and enjoyment without stewardship? They may *enter* marriage, but they cannot fulfill its purpose.

So, they experience dissatisfaction without knowing why. They experience restlessness inside commitment, conflict that feels confusing, or emptiness where depth should be. None of this is because marriage failed but because the covenant was never honored as sacred.

Sacred does not mean grim — it means purposeful. Sacred does not mean joyless. Sacred does not mean heavy all the time. Sacred means this matters, this carries weight. this affects more than me; this answers to God. Marriage can be joyful *because* it is sacred — not in spite of it. But when people want only the fun part, they reduce marriage to consumption.

Covenant cannot survive being consumed. People say, “Marriage didn’t fulfill me.” “It wasn’t what I expected.” “I felt trapped.” “I got bored.” But boredom is not a marriage problem; it’s a purpose problem.

You cannot extract meaning from a covenant you never intended to steward. No covenant in Scripture was made for fun. Pleasure may accompany covenant, but covenant itself is always entered for purpose. When marriage is treated like a toy, people are surprised when it does not behave like a tool.

Marriage is not a playground. It is an altar, and altars are not places you visit casually. They are places you approach with reverence.

People who treat marriage as sacred don’t just *stay married,* they fulfill why marriage exists.

The "fun" that comes of marriage, or any covenant is actually the "rest" because folks are properly aligned and doing what they are supposed to do, with an easy yoke? (Like a toddler just learning to walk -- *Hey look at what I’m doing. Look what I can do.* when toddlers or grown folk are doing 'exploits' that they didn't even know they could do because of Covenant with God.

The "fun" of covenant is not amusement. It is rest. Rest shows up as *joyful capacity*. God put Adam and Eve in the Garden, but it wasn't until after the Fall that they had to strive. Ever since we should have been seeking to enter into His rest. Thank God, Jesus made that possible for us.

Fun is the by-product, not the purpose. In Scripture, rest is never laziness. Rest is alignment.

"Take My yoke upon you… My yoke is easy and My burden is light."

An *easy* yoke doesn't mean *no* work. It means work that fits who you are and how you were made. So when people experience joy, delight, even playfulness inside marriage or covenant, it's not because the covenant exists for fun. It's because they are finally doing what they were designed to do, in the way they were designed to do it.

A toddler learning to walk is not "having fun" because walking is entertainment. They're joyful because something *clicked.* alignment happened. their body is doing what it was made to do. capacity has emerged. They're not performing. They're discovering *"Look what I can do."* That joy is restful joy — not effort-based excitement. That's exactly what happens in covenant done rightly.

Covenant produces exploits, not performances, when people are aligned in covenant: with God, with purpose, with one another. They begin to do things they didn't know they could do endure hardship with Grace, forgive deeply, build something lasting, steward responsibility without resentment, love steadily, not anxiously. Those are *exploits* — not stunts. They feel surprisingly light. Not because they are easy, but because they are right.

Many people chase "fun" as a goal. But fun without alignment becomes exhausting, hollow, compulsive, short-lived. They keep needing more stimulation because there is no rest underneath it.

But when alignment comes first, joy follows naturally. That's why Scripture never commands fun. It commands order, obedience, and covenant.

Joy shows up on its own.

Joy in covenant is not amusement — it is the rest that comes from alignment. What people call 'fun' in marriage is often just the relief of finally walking in what they were designed for. Like a child discovering they can walk, covenant produces joy not because it entertains us, but because it awakens capacity we didn't know we had.

Fun chases pleasure. Rest flows from order. Joy comes from rest, not from fun.

Covenant doesn't promise excitement; it promises fit. When something fits, it feels light — even when it's strong, serious, and weight-bearing.

People often wonder, why do some marriages feel calm and alive, and others feel exhausting? Because one is operating under an easy yoke, and the other is compensating for misalignment. That's not judgment. That's clarity.

Many people enter marriage thinking, "This will make life easier because it will make me happier."

Instead, it is covenant makes life ordered, and happiness emerges as rest. Without this correction, people feel disillusioned and assume something is wrong. Covenant does not exist to entertain us; it exists to align us; alignment produces a joy that feels like rest.

You weren't wrong to want joy--, none of are. You were just told to look for it in the wrong place.

Covenant is about exploits not flesh-ploits. Those who know their God will do exploits (Daniel). But carnal folks are just focusing on the flesh-ploits

The people who know their God shall be strong, and do exploits. (Daniel)

Daniel does not say those who *feel* spiritual, or those who are expressive. It's not about those who indulge desire or those who chase stimulation. It says those who know their God. Covenant--, alignment--, and authority.

Exploits are capacity revealed through alignment. Flesh-ploits are stimulation extracted through appetite. One builds, the other consumes. Carnal focus says, "Look what I can feel." "Look what I can do to satisfy myself. "Look what I can access."

Covenant focus says, "Look what God can do *through* me. "Look what capacity emerges when I'm aligned." Look what becomes possible under authority.

Those are two completely different energies.

People settle for flesh-ploits because they've never been taught that exploits require alignment. Flesh-ploits are immediate. Exploits require governance. Flesh-ploits feel impressive for a moment. Exploits feel *steady* and last. That's why carnality is noisy and covenant is calm.

Flesh-ploits require constant fuel more stimulation, more novelty, more intensity. Exploits emerge from rest right order, right timing, right authority. That's why exploits often surprise the person doing them — like the toddler walking. They didn't *strain* for it. They aligned into it. Those who know their God do exploits; those who do not settle for flesh-ploits — activity without authority, stimulation without alignment.

Exploits flow from covenant; flesh-ploits flow from appetite. Carnal people focus on flesh-ploits. Covenant people discover exploits.

Of course people chase flesh-ploits — they're accessible without alignment. But they are a poor substitute for the joy of discovering what you were actually designed to do.

You do not need a "marriage anointing" in advance. What you need before marriage is self-governance, emotional maturity, covenant alignment, and boundary discipline. The Grace (anointing) to function as a spouse often activates within covenant. All that is different from authority. Marriage authority comes with covenant. Marriage Grace often grows within covenant. They are related, though not identical.

In marriage, authority = covenant jurisdiction. Anointing = Grace to function within it. You don't have marital authority before covenant, but you can and should develop governance before covenant.

Governance is what makes covenant sustainable.

WHEN AUTHORITY IS PROTECTED, NOT DENIED

There are moments in life when something deeply desired does not arrive. Opportunities seem to stall. Relationships do not materialize. Progress feels slower than expected. The natural conclusion many people draw is *"Something is being withheld from me."* But sometimes, what feels like denial is actually protection. Not of comfort. But of authority.

Authority is weight-bearing.

Not everything that is desired can be safely carried at the moment it is wanted. This is difficult to accept because desire feels sincere. But sincerity is not the same as readiness. Delay is often misunderstood. People assume delay means failure, rejection, or lack of favor. But delay is frequently the space where foundations are strengthened quietly. Where governance matures, alignment deepens. Where capacity increases without being noticed.

Refusal closes a door.

Delay prepares you to walk through it without collapse. That is a very different thing. This is why some things in life arrive only after a person has learned patience, restraint, and forgiveness.

It's not so much that God enjoys waiting, but authority must be able to rest on what has been built. Protection often feels like frustration. Because you cannot see what you are being protected from. You only feel what you are being kept from.

But time often reveals that what you thought you needed earlier would have strained you beyond what you could carry. This is especially true in areas like marriage, leadership, influence, and responsibility. These things are not light.

They are structures that depend on authority being stable. And when authority is still being strengthened, protection feels like delay. Understanding this changes how you interpret your timeline. You stop asking, "Why is this not happening yet?" You begin asking, "What is being strengthened in me while I wait?" That shift brings peace where there was once frustration.

Authority is sometimes protected by slowing the pace of your life. By limiting what you can access. By guiding you into smaller spaces where governance can grow. This is not for punishment, but as Mercy. When you see this, you realize something important: You were not being denied; you were being preserved.

What is preserved is able to be carried safely when the time comes. Authority that arrives too early feels overwhelming. Authority that arrives in order feels natural. And often, the difference between the two is the mercy of delay.

SYMBOLS OF AUTHORITY IN SCRIPTURE

These are visual, tangible markers God uses. God repeatedly uses **visible markers** to signal authority.

1. Garments - Priestly robes. Royal garments. Sackcloth (repentance). White robes (restoration)

See **Book of Zechariah 3**. Garments represent *assigned standing*, not personal worth.

2. Names - Adam names creation. Abram → Abraham. Jacob → Israel. Simon → Peter. **Name change = authority shift.**

3. Seat / Throne - Moses' seat. David's throne. Elders at the gate **Seat = right to decide**

4. Staff / Rod / Scepter. Moses' staff. Shepherd's rod. King's scepter. **Delegated power, not inherent power.**

5. Keys - Keys of the Kingdom. Authority to open and shut. **Keys = access control**

6. Seal / Signet Ring - Pharaoh to Joseph. King's decrees. **Seal = executive authority**

7. Table – Provision. Governance. Allegiance. Covenant terms. **Who sets the table defines the authority structure.**

Man has many Authorities, but not unlimited authority. He has multiple, layered stewardships. Loss in one sphere weakens others. Restoration usually happens in order. That's why Jesus confronts: Appetite (wilderness) Allegiance (Mammon). Authority (command, name). Seating (table, kingdom inheritance)

Authority is not additive — it is integrated. When self-governance collapses relational authority distorts. vocational authority corrupts. spiritual authority weakens. Scripture therefore prioritizes obedience before power. character before office. governance before influence.

Man does not hold a single authority, but stewards many — and the loss of one often destabilizes the rest. Authority in Scripture is layered, visible, and entrusted — never autonomous.

For years, people needed to hear *You are not accidental, You are not worthless. You are not forgotten. You are not a joke,*

The Truth is that Man is not merely loved, forgiven, and restored. Man is entrusted, assigned, and held responsible. That's why Hebrews echoes David and sharpens the blade:

"You crowned him with glory and honor and put everything under his feet…"

Man is to be positioned between heaven and earth as a steward.

Man is not questioned because he is weak — he is questioned because he is entrusted. That is why God is mindful of him. That is why Heaven pays attention. That is why authority exists at all.

Man needs to always beware of misuse of authority born from ignorance of value. A passport is a symbol, in the natural, of authority. It gives the owner permission to go from place to place and enter places where there are gates, fences and gatekeepers. But if he takes the passport and burns it; that is misuse. A passport is not warmth. It is not insulation. It is not designed to patch a roof; it is not patch material. It is authorization.

Therefore, a man should not take what grants access to try to solve what requires provision. That's the tragedy.

When a person uses a passport to patch a shoe, tile a roof, burn for heat. They're not being creative, they're being desperate and misaligned. They are solving an immediate need by destroying a long-term authority.

That is exactly what Scripture shows again and again: Esau burns his passport for stew. Judas trades his passport for silver. Adam spends his passport on fruit Jezebel's prophets rent theirs for food, not because they lacked value — but because they lacked discernment of what they were holding.

Man needs authority. Man was created for dominion, crowned with glory and honor--, given authority. Why? Because he needs authority. But if he doesn't know he has it, if he doesn't know what it is, it is at risk. authority doesn't feel like food. It doesn't feel like shelter. It doesn't feel like relief. Authority feels abstract until the moment you need it. Until you need it for access to everyday things, such as situations, condition, and the amenities in life.

Because of authority seeming abstract and intangible, too many times, people sacrifice future passage with that "authority passport" to survive present pressure. That's not stupidity. That's ungoverned hunger.

Authority was never meant to be consumed to solve survival, it was meant to grant access beyond it. We keep burning passports to stay warm, then wondering why we can't leave.

You are not poor; you are misusing what you were given.

There is hope; what was given can be re-governed. Misuse is inevitable if identity collapses into frivolity and why authority gets consumed instead of stewarded.

A MAN UNDER AUTHORITY

This insight: distinguishes stewardship from sonship. It explains why some people plateau clarifies why access $\neq$ trust exposes why proximity doesn't guarantee inheritance

The centurion said, *I am a man under authority....* Biblically a man who has authority is usually set under authority... that's the biblical pattern, and the centurion names it with rare clarity. When the centurion speaks to Jesus Christ, he says: "For I also am a man under authority, having soldiers under me..."(Matthew 8:9) That is jurisdictional logic.

The governing principle from Scripture, is that authority flows through submission, not around it. A man does not gain authority by standing alone. He gains it by being rightly positioned under authority. That's why the centurion understands Jesus immediately: He recognizes rank He understands command. He knows authority does not require proximity or performance. He knows words carry weight only when backed by order.

Adam had authority because he was under God. Moses had authority because he was under God. David had authority because he honored Saul's position. Jesus exercised authority because He was under the Father.

Sons are set under authority before they are entrusted with it. That's why: Judas (never under authority) is entrusted with money. Matthew (submitted) is entrusted with true riches. But I would not have you to be ignorant, brethren, concerning them which are asleep, that ye sorrow not, even as others which have no hope. The centurion recognizes authority instantly. Miracles respond to order, not desperation.

Biblically, men who carry authority are almost always set under authority. The centurion knew something many miss: authority only works when it's rightly ordered. Authority is not independence; authority is alignment.

When the centurion says, "For I also am a man under authority, having soldiers under me…" (Matthew 8:9). He is not describing humility — he is describing how authority works.

The Biblical rule is consistent across Scripture. Authority is not generated by independence. Authority is transmitted through alignment. In Scripture, men who *have* authority are almost always first shown to be set under authority. The centurion understood authority because he lived inside rank and order.

The centurion recognizes Jesus immediately because he knows this law. Authority does not come from proximity, volume, or effort, it comes from right placement. That's why he doesn't ask Jesus to come to his house. He understands that words backed by order are sufficient.

This explains why Judas could handle money but not true riches, why Matthew transformed and was entrusted with revelation, why miracles respond to command, not desperation, and why sonship precedes stewardship. A man who refuses to be governed cannot be trusted to govern.

Biblically, and as a first principle, a man who has authority is usually set under authority. Authority flows through submission, not around it.

FAVOR

There are some who feel that “Something is off.” “Things don’t work like they should.” “I keep losing ground.” “Doors close but I don’t know why.” “I feel displaced in my own life.”

What is really wrong? Is it witchcraft? Ancestral covenants? Familial curses? Iniquity from personal sin. What has happened that changed everything? discipline, sabotage, immaturity, misalignment, culture, trauma, authority void…, or favor.

They just know something is structurally wrong.

And that’s why a brief cultural clarification is wise. Many modern people have only seen authority in three distorted forms: control, charisma, abuse.

They think domination, hierarchy, ego, manipulation. They don’t think stewardship, jurisdiction, alignment, delegated trust. We live in a culture that confuses authority with control and rejects it altogether. But authority is not dominance; it is delegated order. When authority is misunderstood or abdicated, voids form, and disorder follows. Many people sense the disorder but may not know what to call it.

Many who think they have lost favor, have really misnamed the problem; they have lost authority. Mislabeling can lead people to look for the wrong thing to recover and therefore not recover.

Favor and authority are not the same thing. Favor is how others *respond* to you. Authority is where you are *positioned.* Favor is relational and responsive. Authority is jurisdictional and governing. Favor can fluctuate. Authority determines outcomes.

So, when people say, *"Favor has left me,"* what they are often describing is doors no longer opening automatically. people no longer accommodating them. systems no longer bending in their direction. ease giving way to resistance. That doesn't necessarily mean favor is gone. It often means authority has shifted, idled, or moved out of alignment.

It feels like favor left. When authority is functioning properly, favor often follows quietly. things align with less friction. Help appears naturally and resistance feels minimal.

Sometimes, people conflate the two.

When authority is unoccupied, misaligned, outside assignment, deferred through appetite or disengagement, …favor withdraws because it has nothing to respond to. Favor does not initiate, it responds.

Favor is attracted to authority in alignment.

When authority is present and active, favor recognizes it. provision aligns with it. people cooperate with it (sometimes unconsciously). When authority idles favor dissipates. systems stop yielding, resistance increases, and effort multiplies.

- Joseph had favor because authority was operating — even in prison.
- David had favor when aligned — and friction when mispositioned.
- Saul lost favor after authority fractured.
- Jesus grew in favor because He grew in wisdom and stature — governance increasing over time.

Favor didn't leave randomly. Authority shifted first. Calling it "favor" is safer (but less accurate). People prefer to say, "favor left me." When they really should be saying, "I stopped governing something God assigned." Because the first sounds passive. The second requires adjustment.

Recovery doesn't come from chasing favor. It comes from reoccupying authority.

The correct question to ask is not *"How do I get favor back?"* But, "Where did I step out of alignment?" "What authority am I no longer occupying?" "What assignment did I disengage from?" When authority is restored, Favor usually follows — quietly, without announcement.

Favor doesn't usually leave first. Authority does. People say favor left them when what actually happened is that authority idled. Favor follows authority — it doesn't replace it.

Favor is a *response*, not a source. If someone feels like favor is gone, the work is not to plead for favor, No, the answer is to return to governance. Once authority is back in place, favor tends to show up again without being asked.

You will never find what you're looking for, if you are looking for the wrong thing.

God isn't withholding. Perhaps you are mis-aimed. Many people look for favor when what they lost was jurisdiction. Favor is not recovered by pursuit, but by repositioning. Authority restores order; favor responds to order. When authority returns to its place, favor usually follows without effort.

You will never find what is missing, if you're looking for the wrong thing.

THE GOVERNING

In the Gospel of Matthew 26:25, Judas does not address Jesus the same way the other Disciples do in multiple major translations. The key distinction is what the other Disciples say, in earlier verses. In Matthew 26:22, the disciples ask: "Lord, is it I?" The *(Greek, Kyrios — Lord)*. This is a title of authority and submission to that authority.

Major translations render Judas's words: KJV: "Master, is it I?" ESV: "Is it I, Rabbi?" NIV: "Surely you don't mean me, Rabbi?" NASB: "Surely it is not I, Rabbi?" NRSV: "Surely not I, Rabbi?" In the Greek, Judas uses *Rabbi, meaning teacher*. He does not say "Lord."

This is not accidental. Throughout the Gospels, the Disciples increasingly call Jesus "Lord." Judas consistently calls Him "Rabbi." "Rabbi" acknowledges instruction learning proximity but not governance. "Lord" acknowledges authority submission allegiance. Showing that Judas relates to Jesus as one who teaches, not one who governs him. Judas learned from Jesus, but he was never **governed** by Him. Judas called Him Teacher, not Lord—because appetite will learn truth it refuses to obey. The others said 'Lord.' Judas said '*Rabbi.*' That difference tells you everything.

This is why Judas: regretted the outcome, returned the money, and confessed guilt, but did not return allegiance. He never reassigned governance. He learned. He followed. He participated. But he never yielded authority.

Judas couldn't re-assign authority to Jesus because it seems to me that he had never assigned it in the first place. He was in the "Disciples" for his "appetite." You can't re-assign authority you never yielded.

Judas could not return authority to Jesus because he had never placed himself under Jesus' authority in the first place. He was present. He was chosen. He was entrusted. But presence is not submission.

Judas Iscariot consistently relates to Jesus Christ as Teacher (Rabbi), not Lord (*Kyrios*). That's not a linguistic accident. It signals relationship posture. Calling Jesus, teacher, means I learn from you but I am not **governed** by you. Judas accepted instruction. He never accepted governance.

Appetite explains the alignment. Scripture gives repeated clues that Judas's attachment point was provision and access, not allegiance: He kept the money bag. He objected to "wasted" ointment. He negotiated Jesus' betrayal for silver. He returned the money in regret, but not in repentance. His allegiance never matured past benefit.

Regret was possible but repentance was not. Judas regretted the outcome and acknowledged guilt. He tried to undo consequences, but repentance requires something deeper: **the surrender of governance**. You can regret loss without yielding authority. You cannot repent without doing so. That's why his sorrow did not restore him. It's kind of a sorry-not-sorry situation.

Judas did not fail to return authority to Jesus; he revealed that he had never yielded it. He followed for access, not allegiance. Judas couldn't reassign authority because he never assigned it. He stayed for the benefits, not the Lordship.

Many sit close to authority to benefit from it. Many speak its language but never submit to its governance. When belonging is driven by appetite rather than alignment, betrayal is not shocking — it is predictable.

There is no verse that says, Judas healed, or Judas cast out a demon. Nor is it ever said in the regular canonized Bible that Judas performed signs. Unlike Peter, John, or even unnamed disciples, Judas is never individually associated with a miracle in the text.

Scripture does imply when Jesus sends out the Twelve, Judas is included in the group. (Matthew 10:1–8 Mark 6:7–13 Luke 9:1–6). Jesus gives the Twelve authority to: cast out demons, to heal diseases, to preach the Kingdom. In that group, Judas Iscariot is named among the Twelve. Logically, Judas was present when authority was delegated and when the mission occurred. Notice the precision of Scripture: it records the commission it records the group outcome. It never highlights Judas's personal participation or fruit.

Authority can be exercised through proximity without being possessed through allegiance. Authority can flow through someone without being owned by them and without transforming their governance.

Jesus Himself later says: **"Many will say to Me, 'Lord, Lord, did we not prophesy in Your name…?'"** Miraculous activity is not proof of surrendered authority. Scripture never records Judas performing a miracle, even though he was present when authority was delegated. Power may pass through a man who never yields governance to God. Didn't the magicians in Pharaoh's court show signs and snake tricks? All that takes power and allegiance to whatever *god* they are serving.

Judas was trusted with proximity, entrusted with responsibility, exposed to authority, and possibly involved in mission activity. However, Scripture is silent on his fruit — and silence in Scripture is rarely accidental.

WAITING WITHOUT CONSUMING

Waiting is not passive. Waiting is the active preservation of authority. It is the refusal to spend what will be needed later just to feel better now. Waiting feels like loss because appetite interprets restraint as deprivation.

Restraint is not absence. It is guardianship. A man who waits is not doing nothing. He is holding position. He is saying, *I will not trade authority for relief. I will not consume what must be preserved. I will not negotiate under pressure.* That is governance. Authority is preserved in silence. Authority does not announce itself while waiting. It does not posture. It does not argue. It does not demand recognition.

It simply remains intact. This is why waiting is so difficult for appetite. Nothing is happening outwardly, yet everything is being decided inwardly. When a man waits without consuming, something profound occurs: Authority stays where it belongs. No transfer. No negotiation. No loss. The vacancy that appetite opened begins to close — not because something was added, but because order returned.

This is the real turn; it is not behavioral. It is perceptual. The man finally sees that hunger was never his enemy, appetite was never meant to govern, provision was never the exit. Authority was. Authority was never taken from him by force. It was laid down. Which means it can be taken up again — but only through order. Waiting without consuming is not delay. It is the preservation of everything needed to cross the border when release comes.

So, the devil tests folks on authority way more than he tests on sandwiches. but baby steps -- God lets us see (or reach) authority in our ability to handle lesser things like food and mammon.

The enemy is not interested in sandwiches—not so much what we eat. He is interested in authority. Food is just the **training** ground. The devil tests authority far more than appetite — but authority is *revealed* through appetite. That's why Scripture consistently starts with small tests such as food, money, comfort, urgency, or relief. Not because these are the real prizes, but because if a person cannot govern hunger, they cannot be trusted with governance. So, God allows us to *approach* authority through our handling of lesser things. This is not to shame us; it is to train us.

Jesus shows the pattern. The temptation was never: *"Are You hungry?"* It was really, *"Will You use authority prematurely?"*

Bread was just the bait.

Mammon works the same way.

Money is a proxy test. Before authority is entrusted, God watches how we handle provision. He watches how we respond to lack. He looks to see whether urgency makes us compromise. He is seeing and also showing us ourselves if we will but look to see whether relief outruns obedience.

Mammon answers hunger quickly, while authority answers destiny slowly.

The devil tempts authority; God trains it. God doesn't hand authority to people who haven't learned how not to eat it. Food and money are not the issue. They are measuring sticks--, gauges. God is not withholding authority to be cruel. He is protecting it from being consumed instead of exercised.

Authority vs appetite: Jesus vs the Wilderness shows us why people remain stuck even while "provided for. We see why wilderness lasts longer than necessary. How provision can **delay** promotion. Now we know why Satan tempts authority but uses food. And clearly see why Jesus refused to "eat His passport"—His way out of the Wilderness.

THE DIRECTION OF THE WITNESS

Order Matters. It does **not** go both ways equally. Sons do not take identity cues from Creation. Neither does Creation initiate authority. Instead, God gives man the authority to become sons and then Creation will respond accordingly. The son's role is governance. Creation's role is response. So, when Creation shifts, heals, settles, or aligns, it is not crowning sons, but it does confirm them.

Scripture consistently treats **outcomes as evidence**. Fruit bears witness to root. Order bears witness to authority. Peace bears witness to alignment. Creation bears witness to maturity.

That's why Jesus never argued His authority. He let **results testify**. Even in Eternity, our fruit will speak and we are supposed to bear much fruit, and it should remain.

Psalm 19 The Heavens and Earth declare the Glory of God—not the glory of man. Well, not yet, anyway. Sons and creation bear witness to one another; sons by governance; Creation by response. Creation does not recognize titles. It recognizes authority. This is a relationship that Scripture already acknowledges.

Three things in the earth bear witness to one another… The blood, the water and the Spirit or Word … not that familiar with this Scripture.

Creation testifies of son. Sons affect Creation. This is two witnesses, one order.

The child becomes the confidant, the decision partner, the emotional stabilizer, the validator, or the "second self". This is discussed at more length in my book: **Entanglements: *Illegal Knots Limiting Your Life***.

This is not closeness; it's role confusion. It looks as though the child had taken the parent's authority. But that is not what happened. The child has not truly taken the parent's authority, the parent has abdicated it, and the child has been forced to function in its shadow, in that vacuum.

When the child becomes the confidant, the decision partner, the emotional stabilizer, the validator, or the 'second self,' authority is misplaced. It is not transferred. Authority is the right to govern, decide, and carry consequence. Function is the work of stabilizing, advising, and containing.

In role confusion the function moves downward, the authority does *not.* So, the child carries adult emotional weight. manages adult instability. absorbs adult anxiety, …but cannot set boundaries, make final decisions, enforce outcomes, leave without guilt. That's why it's so damaging.

Closeness flows *downward* from authority; it protects the child from adult burden. It increases safety. This is not closeness, it is role confusion flowing *upward* into the child, exposing them to adult vulnerability, and erodes safety. The child appears to hold influence, but not authority; they are made responsible without being empowered. This is not shared leadership — it is abdicated governance. The child is not given authority; they are given weight.

This produces lifelong entanglements.

Children shaped this way grow into adults who confuse emotional labor with love. They often mistake access for intimacy. They feel responsible for other people's stability. They feel disloyal when they choose themselves. Which loops us right back to uncut cords, delayed separation, grief when God enforces distance. Nothing about this is accidental.

The child has been **pressed into service where <u>authority</u> should have stood**.

I was in that conundrum before: I was a stepparent. I had responsibilities but no authority over the kid. Actually no one had authority over the 5-year-old; he was running the house, but I didn't know that until after I had gotten married to the kid's father.

That situation is textbook responsibility-without-authority, and it's destabilizing for *everyone* involved. I was placed in functional responsibility (care, presence, emotional labor), without governing authority (rules, consequences, structure). Meanwhile, the father had **title authority** but did not exercise it. The child sensed the vacuum--, and children *always* fill vacuums. So, the 5-year-old didn't become powerful, although it looked like he had. No, he became **uncontained**.

I was left accountable without power, after all, I'm the "grown-up" in the room. I was blamed without jurisdiction, emotionally invested without agency. That's not marriage. That's misaligned governance.

I didn't see this dysfunctional dynamic until after marriage. Before commitment systems can *appear* functional, gaps are masked by goodwill, novelty, and hope. Authority failures often show up as "quirks" or *adjustments*. After marriage, daily life exposes structure. authority gaps stop being theoretical. responsibility becomes unavoidable. I entered a system that could not reveal itself fully until permanence was introduced. That's not naivety — that's how authority failures work.

*I was asked to help govern what I was never permitted to govern — and the system called that love. I was a w*ell-dressed servant" in that house and marriage.

Servants carry responsibility maintain order, absorb fallout but they do not: set policy correct leadership, override dysfunction. I was given the symbols of authority without the substance of it — expected to serve a system I was never allowed to govern. I wore the ring, but I carried the weight.

A *trophy wife* has symbolic authority, not governing authority — unless the husband deliberately grants and honors real authority.

Authority is the recognized right to decide. The power to set direction and enforce outcomes. The ability to say *no* and have it respected. Symbolic status. Visibility, Prestige, Representation, Access without jurisdiction. A trophy wife is elevated in appearance, not in governance.

So, what authority does a trophy wife usually have? she *may* have Social influence (how the couple is perceived) Curated voice (approved opinions, safe topics). Domestic delegation (execution of plans already decided)

She usually does *not* have: Final say over finances. Authority over children's discipline. Power to correct or confront the husband. Jurisdiction over the household's moral direction. Freedom to disrupt appearances. If her authority disappears the moment she disagrees, she didn't have authority — she had permission.

Authority is proven by what happens when you disagree.

If disagreement costs Peace, safety, or standing — authority was never present.

THE AUTHORITY LITMUS TEST

(This works for marriage, parenting, work, ministry — everything.)

You can tell who has authority by answering **these questions**, honestly. **1. What happens when I say "no"?** Is "no" respected? Or am I pressured, punished, overridden, or emotionally managed? If "no" triggers consequences, you don't have authority — you have permission.

2. Can I change outcomes — or only manage reactions? Can I redirect decisions? Or am I expected to make bad decisions feel better?

Authority changes direction.

Labor manages damage.

3. Who carries consequences when things go wrong? Do I absorb blame for decisions I didn't make? Do I clean up messes I couldn't prevent? Responsibility without authority is exploitation — even when it's dressed nicely.

4. Am I consulted before decisions are made — or informed after? Is my input formative? Or ceremonial? Being "heard" is not the same as being *heeded.*

5. Can I enforce boundaries without retaliation? Do my boundaries stabilize the system? Or destabilize my standing? Authority protects boundaries. Systems without authority punish them.

6. Who is protected by the structure — me or the image? When conflict arises, does truth win? Or does appearance? If the image is protected at your expense, authority is cosmetic.

7. If I step back, does the system collapse? If yes, you were carrying weight, not authority. If no, authority is actually functioning elsewhere. Authority sustains systems *without* exhausting individuals.

When authority is weak, delayed, abdicated, or emotionally compromised, a son will attempt to self-appoint as ruler — either by force, manipulation, or rivalry.

Absalom (son of David) Absalom's takeover was: political, emotional, public. He didn't just want inheritance — he wanted the throne while the father still lived.

How?

He positioned himself as the one who understands the people. He undermined trust in David's judgments. He exploited unresolved injustice (Tamar / Amnon). He gathered loyalty *before* authority was transferred. This is the classic takeover spirit. It says, *"If authority won't govern, I will."*

Adonijah – another of David's sons, exalted himself. declared himself king. gathered support, did this while David was still alive. Scripture makes a chilling note, *"His father had never displeased him at any time by saying, 'Why have you done so?'"* That's authority failure. Adonijah didn't rebel against authority; he grew up without encountering it.

Esau wanted *birthright power* without *birthright responsibility*. He despised inheritance discipline. He resented Jacob's acquisition of authority. He defaulted to physical dominance. Different method than Absalom, cut it was the same impulse: *"I should have the position because I'm the stronger one."*

Joseph is important because he did NOT seize authority. He received vision, endured delay, submitted to unjust systems, waited for God to confer authority lawfully. That's why his rise didn't fracture the house permanently — it *preserved* it.

These cases have in common The father's authority was emotionally compromised, inconsistently exercised, delayed, or avoided. Then the son's response was self-appointment, rivalry, manipulation, or open challenge. The issue was not ambition alone, it was ambition in an ungoverned environment.

Absalom is not merely rebellious, narcissistic, ambitious. He is the fruit of a system where. authority was symbolic. justice was delayed. confrontation was avoided.

Responsibility without authority creates chaos. So does sonship without governance. When a father will not govern, a son will eventually attempt to replace him — not because he is evil, but because the house cannot remain unruled.

Absalom didn't invent the takeover spirit. He perfected it. And Scripture keeps recording it because it's not about sons — it's about authority vacuums.

Reuben belongs in this pattern, but in a very specific way. He represents failed primacy, not a successful takeover. Reuben: firstborn without authority fulfillment. Reuben (son of Jacob). Reuben was the firstborn, legally positioned for authority, entitled to **inheritance leadership.** But Jacob says of him:

Unstable as water, thou shalt not excel. (Genesis 49:4)

Reuben had position, but not governance. Reuben did not attempt a coup like Absalom. Instead, he tried to intervene *weakly* (Joseph). acted impulsively (Bilhah). never consolidated leadership among his brothers. So his failure was not aggression — it was **instability**. Authority cannot rest on instability.

Reuben lost authority through boundary violation. Sleeping with his father's concubine wasn't just sexual sin. It was a symbolic invasion of the father's domain. a violation of generational order. I was an assertion without governance. In authority language, He crossed a boundary he did not have jurisdiction to cross.

That disqualified him.

Absalom seized authority prematurely. Reuben squandered authority carelessly. Different expressions, with the same result: authority transfer bypassed them. "thou shalt not excel" is precise. To *excel* means to rise. to be preeminent. to surpass. Jacob is saying, *You will not rise into what your position promised.*

That's devastating — because Reuben *could have risen to his rightful position, rightfully.* Authority was available. Character was not ready. Reuben did not lose authority because he was not chosen — he lost it because he could not steward what was already his. Being first does not guarantee governance.

All three, Absalom, Adonijah, and Reuben show that authority is not automatic. It must be governed, restrained, and honored. Absalom answers: *What happens when authority is absent?* Reuben answers: *What happens when authority is mishandled?*

MATTHEW: TRUE RICHES

The governing principle is shown here. Matthew was entrusted with true riches. Judas was entrusted with money. That contrast is not accidental.

Jesus Himself defines true riches: **"If therefore ye have not been faithful in the unrighteous mammon, who will commit to your trust the true riches?"** (Luke 16:11)

Scripture already gives us the categories: Mammon for money, access, provision True riches for authority, revelation, stewardship of the Kingdom.

Matthew qualified but Judas did not. Matthew: relinquished his former authority (tax booth) submitted to Jesus' governance underwent transformation was entrusted with testimony, witness, and truth became a steward of revelation (a Gospel) That is sonship-level trust.

Judas: retained control over money never yielded governance measured value constantly handled provision but not authority. Judas was never entrusted with revelation. Money is money but true riches is both durable and everlasting.

The issue is not competence, it is allegiance. Without authority, men do not transform into sons of God, and they are not entrusted with true riches. Men are not entrusted with true riches until authority has been surrendered. Without authority, there is no transformation into sonship. Money can be managed without authority, but true riches are only entrusted to sons.

Authority level correlates to *pay grade.*

1. **Level** – not all authority is the same
2. **Limits** – you can't authorize what you're not assigned
3. **Timing** – pay grades change with role, maturity, and trust

Authority is real, but it has levels. Jurisdiction is tied to your current pay grade. Some things are above your pay grade—not forever, just not yet. You may see the problem clearly, but that decision may be above your current *pay grade.* God doesn't give authority all at once. He assigns it by role, season, and trust—like pay grade. Trying to operate above your pay grade doesn't make you powerful. It makes you exposed.

Acting above their pay grade can be described as people reaching beyond their assignment, act outside jurisdiction and confuse insight with authority.

CONCLUSION

By now, you have seen that authority is not loud. It is not aggressive. It is not something you seize. It is not something you perform. Authority is something you are entrusted with, something you learn to steward, something you may set down without realizing, and something you can return to through alignment.

You have seen that authority rests on identity, boundaries, autonomy, governance, covenant, and alignment. It is not dependent or supported on personality, force, or effort. Understanding changes how you see yourself.

You begin to realize that your life carries weight not because you are impressive, but because you have been trusted with something. That realization does not feel heavy. It feels dignified. Many people avoid seriousness because they think it is a burden. They think it means pressure, responsibility, and strain. But seriousness, in the Biblical sense, is simply the recognition that your life is not casual. It has meaning, consequence, and purpose.

That is not a burden. That is dignity.

God restores authority carefully because authority is meant to be safe in your hands. He does not rush it. He does not force it. He does not overwhelm you with it. He allows it to grow as you grow. He allows it to return as you realign. He allows it to rest where it can be trusted.

This is why authority, when understood properly, brings peace instead of pressure. You stop trying to prove yourself. You stop trying to rush your life. You stop trying to control outcomes. You begin to steward what is in front of you with steadiness.

Authority that can be trusted does not make you loud. It makes you calm. It does not make you domineering. It makes you stable. It does not make you urgent. It makes you patient. And when you begin to live this way, something changes quietly.

Your words carry weight again. Your decisions feel clearer. Your life feels ordered instead of reactive. Not because you have gained something new. But because you have returned to what was always entrusted to you. You are not a toy. You are not a joke. You are not an accident. You are entrusted. When you understand that, you begin to live like a person whose authority can be trusted. Every day and every night can be defined if you are in your authority.

When a person is not in authority (self-governance, alignment, covenant order), days feel reactive, accidental, driven by mood, shaped by other people.

Night feels restless, anxious, escapist, compensatory. But when someone is standing in authority The day has intention. The night has rest. Decisions have boundaries. Reactions have restraint.

Authority doesn't eliminate difficulty. It eliminates drift. That's what "defined" really means. Even Biblically, creation is structured this way Evening and morning — one day.

Definition precedes flourishing.

Light separated from darkness. Waters separated from waters. Boundaries established first. Authority seeks order and defines before it governs. When you are in your authority, even sorrow is defined. Waiting is defined. Even descent is defined. You are not lost inside your own life. That's why authority produces Peace. Not because everything is easy, but because everything has order.

Jesus, our ultimate passport. A passport grants access. It establishes identity and citizenship. It authorizes lawful entry. It is order. Christ is our access, He is our citizenship, our standing and our reconciliation, That's consistent with Ephesians 2; access through Him.

But Jesus is not merely a tool of access. He is not a credential we carry; He is Lord. Authority does not come from "using" Jesus. Authority flows from union and alignment with Him.

Misuse happens when people treat Jesus like a passcode, a formula, a badge to flash, a name to drop or invoke mechanically--, that's mislabeling and misusing. It turns relationship into instrument, and that's dangerous.

Not with eyeservice, as menpleasers; but as the servants of Christ, doing the will of God from the heart (Ephesians 6:6)

Christ is not a passport we wield, but the Lord under whom we stand. We do not use Jesus to exercise authority; we align with Him, and authority flows from that alignment. You cannot fake authority.

Passports can be burned. Credentials can be misapplied. Names can be dropped to sway or impress. Names can be invoked wrongly. But Christ is not an object of authorization; He is the source and Sovereign of it. Mislabeling Him as a mechanism instead of Lord leads to distortion not real authority.

You cannot fake authority.

Dear Reader

Thank you for acquiring and reading this book, I pray it has blessed you to better understand AUTHORITY of every kind and how to be in right alignment to walk in your God-given, Divine Authority.

Shalom,

Dr. Marlene Miles

If you enjoyed this book, here are some new releases by this author.

Christ of God (*The*) 3-book series

Christ of God, (*The*) Box Set, includes all three books

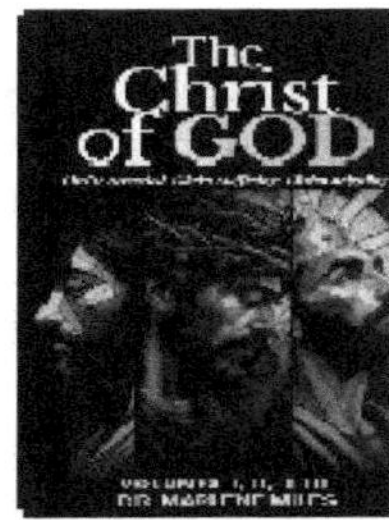

Other books on Authority:

<u>Entanglements: *Illegal Knots Limiting Your Life,*</u>

<u>How a Man Is Owned,</u> <u>Ungoverened Hunger,</u> <u>Tribe</u>

Dr. Marlene Miles has many other titles. They are available on Amazon and many other platforms.

www.ingramcontent.com/pod-product-compliance
Lightning Source LLC
LaVergne TN
LVHW010947110826
845149LV00015B/3250
9781971933252